THE **SMART** SALES SYSTEM

The **SMART** Sales System

SELL SMARTER, NOT HARDER

By Michael Halper

ISBN: 978-0-578-61576-9

Table of Contents

CHAPTER 1

Introduction

Welcome to the SMART Sales System! Today is the first day of the rest of your life. I say that because if you implement this system, you will not only sell more, but selling will actually become easier and more enjoyable. To take the first step of introducing the system to you, I will start by answering three questions:

1. What does SMART stand for?
2. In what way is this a system?
3. What can you expect from this?

What Does SMART Stand For?

If you are a salesperson, there are many different sales tools that will help you to sell more:

- Computer, laptop, and tablet
- Office phone and cell phone
- Internet access and Wi-Fi hotspot
- Email account
- CRM
- Social media accounts
- Email automation and marketing software

While all of these sales tools will help you to sell more, I believe the most important and powerful sales tool you have is what you say when talking with prospects. For example, you can have the best email marketing software, but if you don't know what to say in your email messages, the software will not help you much.

That is why our mission is to help you to communicate in the clearest and most optimum way when prospecting, and this is exactly what the SMART Sales System is designed to do. To begin to explain how it does that, let's start with what SMART stands for:

SALES MESSAGING AND RESPONSE TACTICS

- **Sales Messaging:** Your sales messaging is the set of talking points and questions that you use when communicating with prospects on the phone, in emails, at networking events, in meetings, in presentations, in proposals, etc. The SMART Sales System will help you to build your sales message and tell you exactly what you could say in all of these different situations.

- **Response:** The SMART Sales System will help you with how to respond to prospect objections and questions. Not only will the system teach you a methodology for figuring out how to respond to prospects, but it will also provide you with actual responses that you can use.

- **Tactics:** The SMART Sales System will provide actual tactics for what to do and say in all of the common prospecting situations that you will find yourself in.

In What Way Is This a System?

We use the word system because this is not just a sales training program that will provide you with a bunch of tips. It is actually filled with processes and steps to follow, making it a system that you can implement and adopt for yourself or for your sales organization. I have attended many different sales training programs and read dozens of books on how to sell, and while every book and training program will have insightful information and tips, most of them are not easy to implement or adopt. There were multiple occasions where I listened to a speaker or attended a workshop and felt either inspired or intrigued by the topics presented. Yet, on every occasion when I returned to my desk and it was time to pick up the phone, I was not in a better place with knowing what to do or how to implement the new information that I had learned.

I think there are two reasons why a lot of sales training materials are difficult to adopt and implement.

All Fluff

A lot of sales training materials might be entertaining, motivating, and even inspiring, but they have no real substance or direction in terms of telling you what you need to do. An example of this could be listening to a motivational speaker who tells amazing stories that pump you up and make you feel inspired. But the next day when you are back at your desk, you may be right back where you were before listening to the speaker.

Too Complex

Some sales training materials are on the other end of the spectrum and have too much complexity and detail. For these, you can find some valuable advice and tips, but the suggestions are too complicated to implement and adopt. For example, one book that I read had a nine square matrix that you were supposed to fill out with prospects in appointments. I really liked the matrix and what it tried to get you to find out about the prospect, but it was complicated figuring out how to go through it with a prospect in real life. As a result, I loved the concept in a book, but I have never used that sales tactic with a prospect.

When you have a sales training program that falls into either of those categories, you might not end up changing what you do, and this greatly reduces the return on investment (ROI) for the time and money that is spent learning the new information.

We solve that issue and are different from those sales training programs in three main ways.

THE SYSTEM WILL TELL YOU WHAT TO DO

With the SMART Sales System, you do not have to worry about getting back to your desk and not knowing what to do as the system will tell you exactly what to do in all of the common sales situations you will find yourself in. For example, when prospecting you will be sending emails, making calls, talking to gatekeepers, facing objections, hosting meetings, etc. The system will tell you what to do and say in all of these situations and more.

THE SYSTEM IS PRACTICAL AND EASY TO IMPLEMENT

All of the tips, tactics, and processes that the SMART Sales System recommends are very practical and easy for you to implement. In other words, they are very small changes that you can easily make regardless of your level of experience, sales skills, educational background, or personality.

THE SYSTEM INCLUDES A SOFTWARE APPLICATION

One of the keys to successfully implementing a sales training program is to continue to reinforce the concepts learned. If you do not continue to think about and try to use what you learned, there is a good chance that you will forget a lot of the suggestions and tips and just go back to what you were doing before you were exposed to the new information.

What is good about the SMART Sales System is that it has a software application called SalesScripter that completely aligns with all of the tips, processes, and concepts that are in the underlying sales methodology. After learning the sales methodology, you can use the SalesScripter software application as part of your daily routine. This not only makes it easy for you to implement the sales methodology, but it also reinforces what you learned, improving the retention and adoption of the sales training material.

What You Can Expect from All of This

We are confident that if you adopt and implement this system, you will become a SMART salesperson. But what does that mean exactly? Let's break it down.

You will know what to do: The system will help you to know what to do and say in many of the different sales situations that you will encounter, and this will make you feel SMARTer.

You will make a better impression: Since you will know what to say, you will communicate better, and that will help you to appear SMARTer and improve the impression you make with sales prospects.

Establish more conversations: Because you are communicating better and making better impressions, it will be easier for you to establish conversations and get your foot in the door of more accounts.

Have better interactions: You will know what questions to ask, and this will help you to get more information from prospects and get the most out of every interaction.

Build more rapport: By making a better impression and having better interactions, you will improve your ability to build rapport with prospects.

Make SMARTer decisions: By having more information about your prospects, you will be able to make SMARTer decisions throughout the entire sales process. You will have more clarity as to which prospects to pursue and which ones to walk away from. This will help you to be SMARTer with how you manage your valuable time.

Generate more leads: By being able to make better impressions, get into more conversations, get the most out of each interaction, build more rapport, and make SMARTer decisions, you will likely generate more leads and build a healthier pipeline. This will allow you to be more confident and SMARTer with how you forecast and control opportunities in your pipeline.

Selling will become easier: When you make better impressions with prospects and build more rapport, you will face less objections, reluctance, and unresponsiveness, and this will make selling feel easier and less stressful.

Anxiety will decrease: By becoming SMARTer and knowing what to say and do, you will be more confident and competent. This will decrease the amount of anxiety you have with making phone prospecting calls, meeting with prospects, and delivering presentations.

How to Read This Book

This book is organized into three main sections:

1. Sales Message (Sales Pitch)
2. Sales Tools (Scripts and Templates)
3. Sales Tactics and Processes (Tips)

SECTION 1—SALES MESSAGE (SALES PITCH)

The first section will help you to build your sales message. We will take you through each of the following areas to provide a step-by-step process to help you brainstorm and organize the best things to say.

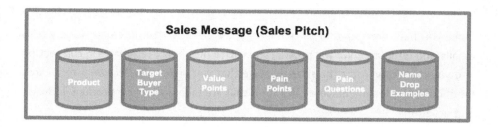

It is probably best to brainstorm how these concepts apply to you and create your sales message as you read each chapter of Section 1. Not only will this prevent you from having to go back through all of these chapters again after you finish the book, but when you go through the second and third sections of the book, the concepts might make more sense if you created your sales message because you will be able to picture everything being discussed as it applies to your particular situation.

If you plan to create your message as you read the chapters of Section 1, at a minimum, try to have a pad of paper and pen with you so that you can make some notes. If you want to be a little more thorough and organized, have your computer next to you with a document or spreadsheet open. As you think of how the concepts apply to you, put your ideas and thoughts in the document or spreadsheet and this will make it easier for you to edit the information later and create some of the documents that are provided in Section 2.

However, the most optimum way to do this is to create your sales message in the SalesScripter software application because the software completely aligns with the book. Each step that the book takes you through is a step in the software application. One key benefit to using the software in parallel with the book is that all of the scripts and tools that are provided in Section 2 of the book are already loaded in the software. By creating your sales message in the software, the system will load your message into the library of documents, and this will save you a tremendous amount of time by not having to create all of the different scripts, emails, and templates. For more information on the SalesScripter software application, visit www.salesscripter.com.

SECTION 2—SALES TOOLS (SCRIPTS AND TEMPLATES)

Once you have created your sales message, we can use that to create your scripts, emails, and templates. We will provide you with a number of templates in this section, and you can easily insert the sales message that you created in Section 1 to create a lot of different documents and sales tools that are tailored to your product, industry, and situation.

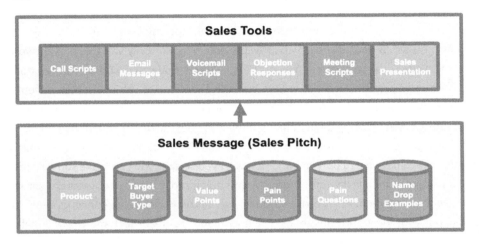

This section of the book is primarily a library of documents. With that, it is not the type of chapters that you will read from beginning to end. More so, it is a set of chapters that is designed for you to flip through so that you can see what is there and what you can use later when you are prospecting. And when you finish reading the book, this section should serve as document repository that you come back to on an ongoing basis to grab scripts, emails, and templates.

SECTION 3—SALES TACTICS AND PROCESSES (TIPS)

The third section of the book provides tips, tactics, and processes that you can use when prospecting. A lot of what is discussed in this section will explain how to use the sales message and sales tools that are created in the first two sections. For example, in one of the chapters in Section 2, we provide an entire set of objection responses. In

Section 3, we provide a methodology for how to respond to objections and how to use all of the responses that are provided in Section 2.

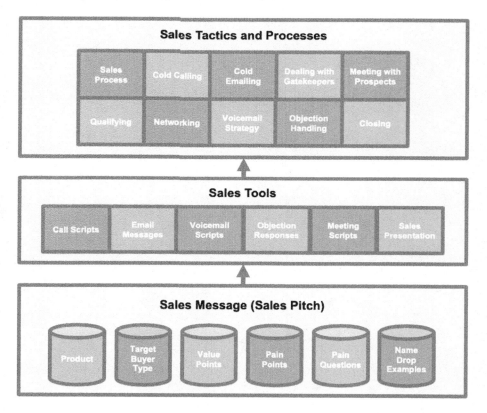

CHAPTER 2

Core Concepts

We are going to discuss a lot of tips, tactics, and processes in this book. But before we get to those, it is important to go through some core concepts. Just about every chapter and area that we discuss in this book will be impacted by or associated with these core concepts.

Understand the Prospect

When dealing with other people in any type of conflict, disagreement, or sensitive situation, you greatly improve your ability to figure out how best to deal with the other people by trying to understand where they are coming from or their particular situation. This could be as simple as just taking a few seconds to try to think about what the other person is going through, what he or she wants and why, what that person cares about, etc.

One of the reasons this is helpful is that in interpersonal situations, you are basically making a lot of small and very quick decisions regarding what to do (and not to do) and what to say (and not say). When you can understand the other person's situation, you have additional information to base these small decisions on, and that can help you to have more clarity on what to do and not do. By trying to understand the other person better, it might not change what you ultimately want or try to do, but it could have an impact on how you communicate and deal with the other person.

Prospects Are Extremely Busy

As you try to understand sales prospects better, the first thing to understand is that they are most likely extremely busy, especially if you are calling at a decision maker level. This is important because it can sometimes seem impossible to get your target prospects to answer the phone. And when this continually happens, you can begin to think prospects are avoiding your call and that they are not interested. But the reality could very well be that they are simply away from their desk in meetings or traveling every time you call. Staying aware of this can play a role in how many times you reach out to prospects and what you say when you reach out, and we will talk about both of those throughout this book.

Prospects Get Sold to a Lot

Another thing to understand about your prospects is that they have a lot of other salespeople who are calling and emailing them every day. And the higher you go in an organization, the worse this is. Their phones and email have a steady flow of contact attempts from salespeople just like you all day. This means that your calls, emails, and voicemails are part of this larger noise that prospects are hearing every day. Not only does this drown out your message, but it can also make prospects more guarded and annoyed.

Don't Sound Like a Salesperson

If you agree that a lot of salespeople reaching out to your prospects can make them guarded and annoyed, then the worst thing that you can do is give off the impression that you are a salesperson who is trying to sell something as this could lead to more objections and rejection. With that logic, if you can minimize how much you look like a salesperson who is trying to sell something, you can minimize the level of difficulty and resistance that you face with prospects.

Focus on Their Interests, Not Yours

We are all a little self-absorbed. And with that, we usually care more about the things we are interested in and what impacts us personally. For example, if one of your hobbies is playing tennis, you will likely enjoy spending time playing, watching, and even talking about tennis. But if your friend likes to play golf and you do not, you will likely find it boring when your friend wants to play, watch, and talk about golf. If you and your friend were to spend time together and were going to talk about or watch a particular sport on TV, you would likely find it more interesting and enjoyable if that sport was the one you are interested in, which is tennis.

If you agree with this logic, you can use it to your advantage to build better relationships by focusing on the other person's interests. For example, if you get together with a friend for lunch, if you can focus a lot of the conversation on his or her interests—kids, career, vacation, relationships, hobbies, etc.—you can increase engagement in the conversation and how much your friend enjoys talking with you.

Applying this to business-to-business (B2B) sales, a salesperson and a prospect typically have different interests. While salespeople are interested in their product and company, prospects are interested in their own company, career, and job. With that, when salespeople talk primarily about the product they sell and the company they work for, they are focusing on their own interests, and these are not the interests of the prospects. This can make it more difficult to grab the prospect's attention and create an engaging conversation. In the same way that someone might be bored having lunch with you if you only talk about your interests and hobbies, a prospect will be less responsive and interested if the salesperson only focuses on his or her own interests.

To use that dynamic to your advantage, focus more on the prospect in your messages, calls, and meetings and resist the natural instinct to focus on your own interests, and we will explain how to do that throughout this book.

The Best Salesperson Asks the Best Questions

It is my personal belief that the best salesperson is the one who asks the best questions. Not only does asking good questions help to extract valuable information that you can use throughout the sales process, but it also makes all of your interactions more engaging. Asking questions also helps you to focus more on the prospect's interests, and it is the easiest way to get a conversation centered around the prospect and what he or she cares about.

However, you might agree and want to ask more questions when talking with prospects, but not be completely clear on what questions to ask. Do not worry as the

SMART Sales System will make it extremely clear what questions to ask when talking with sales prospects.

Prospects Are Likely Not in Buying Mode

When performing cold prospecting and sales outreach, it is good to assume that your prospects are not in "buying mode" at the time when you call or send your email. We are not saying that they do not need what you sell. More so, we are saying that it is most likely the case that when they receive your call or email, there is a fairly low probability that they are thinking about buying what you sell at that exact time. This mismatch is not a big concern or reason for you to not reach out to these prospects. But it is something that you should be aware of and can factor into what you say when reaching out to prospects.

Don't Sell the Product, Sell the Meeting

There is a common saying you will hear in the world of sales of "Always Be Closing." While I fully agree with this way of thinking, I think it is critical to be aware of what you are actually trying to close at all of the different steps of the sales process. What I mean by that is there are always two different things you can close for:

1. **The ultimate goal:** This is getting the prospect to agree to purchase your product or service.

2. **The immediate goal:** This is getting the prospect to agree to move to the next step in your sales process.

This is extremely important because it is our natural instinct to always be trying to close the prospect on the ultimate goal. Even if we have a twelve to eighteen-month sales process or sales cycle, we still communicate in a way where we are focused on closing for the ultimate goal every time we call, email, and meet with a prospect. For example, a payroll salesperson once asked me on a cold call if we were looking at making a change for payroll processing. While that sounds like a logical question to ask, it is actually aligned with her ultimate goal as it has more to do with me buying the service she was selling. In order to sell payroll outsourcing, she will likely need to take me through some sort of process that has at least a few conversations and sales process steps. As a result, the immediate goal for this salesperson would be to close for the next step in her sales process, which might be to schedule an appointment. If she resisted the natural instinct to focus on the ultimate goal and simply focused more on the immediate goal and closing for an appointment or conversation, there might be better questions to ask that could have simply started the conversation or found a reason to talk more on another day.

This concept impacts how you move prospects through your sales process, the questions you ask, how you deal with objections, and how you close. We will discuss all of those areas throughout this book, but the point here is to resist that natural instinct of closing for the ultimate goal and focus more on simply getting the prospect to agree to the next step of the sales process. In other words, focus more on selling the meeting instead of trying to sell the product.

LEVEL 1—SALES MESSAGE

CHAPTER 3

Consultative Selling

The SMART Sales System is built around a consultative selling approach. This detail is important as it impacts every chapter, concept, and tip that we discuss in this book. With that, it is important to explain what we mean when we say consultative selling, and I will do that in this chapter.

Product Selling

Before we talk about what consultative selling is, I want to start out by talking about what most salespeople do, and that is product selling. This is an approach where a salesperson primarily talks about his or her product when talking with prospects and tries to talk prospects into wanting the product. Which at first glance, this sounds like the logical approach—you have a product to sell, so go out and talk about your product. But the problem with this approach can become more apparent when you factor in some of the core concepts we discussed in the last chapter:

- Prospects get sold to a lot
- Don't sound like a salesperson
- Focus on their interests, not yours
- Prospects are likely not in buying mode

If you combine a product selling approach with those core concepts, you can increase situations where there is either a conflict or mismatch with what the salesperson is trying to do and where the prospect is at. This can create missed opportunities and increase the level of resistance that the salesperson faces on a daily basis.

And while a product selling approach is not optimum, it is actually very understandable for a salesperson to sell in this way because it is more aligned with our natural instincts. If you work for a company and were hired to sell a product or service, it is only natural for you to try to generate sales by talking about your product as much as you can. This is also how a lot of companies train their salespeople as they will put new sales hires through a sales training program that primarily teaches details about the products they will be selling. When the training is complete, the salesperson will be given a territory and a quota and told to go sell. It is only natural for a salesperson to take all of their newly gained product knowledge and then try to sell by primarily talking about his or her product when interacting with prospects.

To be clear, I am not saying that this is horrible or that you can't be successful with this approach. I just feel that this approach is like trying to swim upstream with all of the forces against you that were outlined in the last chapter on core concepts. In my opinion, there is a better approach, one where you will not face so much resistance and it will be the equivalent of swimming with the current, and I will explain that next.

Consultative Selling

Instead of trying to talk prospects into wanting your product, I believe a better approach is to focus on trying to find the prospects who need what you sell and then solve that need by providing your product. Part of the logic here is that if you create a pie chart of all prospects, there will be a slice of the pie that is prospects who need what you sell.

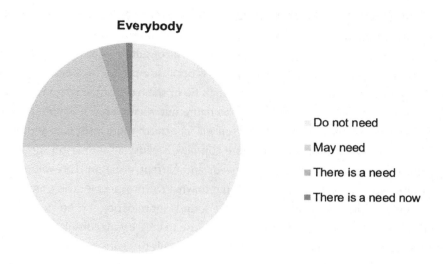

Everybody

- Do not need
- May need
- There is a need
- There is a need now

Because a product selling salesperson is more focused on talking about his or her product, they might end up trying to sell to prospects that are in all of the different slices of this pie. This can lead to more resistance, rejection, wasted time, poor quality leads, and prospects that are difficult to close.

A consultative selling salesperson will use a different approach that focuses more on the prospect and tries to learn about his or her needs. This will help the salesperson to determine which slice of the pie the prospect falls into. If the prospect is in a slice that does not need the product, the consultative selling salesperson might decide to save everybody's time and move on to try to find a different prospect who is a better fit. The consultative selling approach accomplishes this by asking good questions out of the gate. Not only does this focus the conversation more on the prospect's interests, but it will also make the salesperson look more like a consultant or advisor than someone that who is trying to sell something.

After a consultative selling salesperson determines that the prospect fits well with the product being sold, he or she can then begin to introduce the product as a solution to the prospect's problems or needs.

Creating a Consultative Selling Sales Message

Another reason that most salespeople lean toward product selling is that it is actually easier to be a product selling salesperson than a consultative selling salesperson when it comes to figuring out what to say. This is because a product selling salesperson can just improvise and rely on product details he or she has learned when talking with a prospect. However, while it is easier to figure out what to say, it is not an easier approach overall because this salesperson will face much more resistance and rejection.

Consultative selling can be more complex because a salesperson should talk to a prospect more about his or her needs and current situation. This will require the salesperson to ask good questions, listen to what the prospect is saying, and talk more about benefits and pain points. If that sounds intimidating, do not worry. We will provide a very simple process that you can use to create your consultative selling sales message. Once you have that, it will not be difficult to figure out what to say because you will have the key questions to ask and points that to make. While this may take a little effort and time on the front-end, this approach will be easier overall than product selling because you will face much less resistance and rejection when talking with prospects.

COMPONENTS TO A CONSULTATIVE SELLING SALES MESSAGE

We have broken the consultative selling sales message into these different topics that you can discuss with prospects.

- **Product:** These are the key details about the product you sell. This can include details about features, functionality, differentiation, ROI, impressive company facts, etc.

- **Value Points:** These are the improvements that your prospects are likely to see if they use your product.

- **Pain Points:** These are the problems that your product can help prospects to resolve, minimize, or avoid.

- **Pain Questions:** These are questions that you can ask prospects to see if they have or are concerned about any of the pain points that your product helps to resolve, minimize, or avoid.

- **Name-Drop Examples:** These are examples of how your product has helped your customers.

The process that we will take you through will help you to brainstorm and develop key points to say in each of those categories. Once you have that, it will be very easy to mix and match all of those talking points to create a number of different scripts, emails, and sales tools, all of which will help you to know exactly how to be a consultative selling salesperson and what to say in all of the different sales prospecting situations.

Demonstration with an Example

To show how moving from product selling to consultative selling can help you, I would like to use a quick example of a salesperson who sells memberships to a health and fitness club.

PRODUCT SELLING APPROACH

If a prospect walks through the door of the club and is greeted by a product selling salesperson, the salesperson might start the sales process with a tour of the facility where he or she will show the product:

- *We have free weights.*
- *We have weight machines.*
- *We have thirty treadmills.*
- *We have a yoga studio.*
- *We have a full schedule of group classes.*
- *We have two pools.*
- *We have a dry sauna and steam room.*

After showing the product, the salesperson will likely then go straight for the close by sharing the different membership packages.

CONSULTATIVE SELLING APPROACH

If we change that scenario to a consultative selling salesperson, the salesperson may start the process by spending anywhere between fifteen to thirty minutes asking the prospect questions to learn about his or her needs, interests, and challenges as a first step. This does a few powerful things:

- This makes it more about the prospect than about the product or the salesperson.

- It allows the salesperson to tailor the rest of the discussion and sales process according to the prospect's needs.

- This creates a more consultative impression, which will help to build more rapport and trust.

After learning about the prospect, the consultative selling salesperson can then show the product by taking the prospect on a tour. Unlike the product selling salesperson, this salesperson can tailor the tour (demonstration) according to what the prospect is most interested in and needs.

The consultative selling salesperson will not just talk about the product; he or she will talk about the improvements the product will make for the prospect. For example, instead of just talking about weights, machines, and classes, this salesperson will talk about:

- Getting healthier
- Improving self-esteem
- Decreasing stress and depression
- Improving personal relationships
- Life transformation

Which salesperson do you think will be best positioned to sell more? The one who talks about weights and machines or the one who talks about transforming someone's life?

In order to be more of a consultative salesperson, you first need to have a consultative selling sales message as this will help you to have clarity around what questions to ask, what points to emphasize, and how to respond in certain situations. In the next few chapters, we will take you through a step-by-step process that you can use to create your consultative selling sales message.

CHAPTER 4

Product

The first step in creating your consultative selling sales message is to identify the product that you want to build your sales message around.

What We Mean by "Product"

In the SMART Sales System, when we use the term "product", we are simply referring to what it is that you are trying to sell. Whether you sell a physical product, a service, or a group of products or services, everything that we discuss in this book and methodology will be applied in the exact same way. Whenever we refer to "your product", simply insert the product, service, or group of products or services that you are trying to sell.

Make a List of What You Sell

You may know right away which product you want to build your sales message around. But whether that is the case or not, a good first step to take is to brainstorm to create a list of the different things that you sell.

PRODUCTS AND SERVICES

To demonstrate how to brainstorm what you sell, if I use the health and fitness club example from the last chapter, I might end up with a list that looks something like this:

- Gym membership
- Personal training
- Vitamins and supplements
- Nutrition consulting

FEATURES

Try to brainstorm some of the main features of the products or services that you sell. These are some of the features of the health and fitness club product:

- Free weights and machines
- Treadmills, exercise bikes, elliptical machines
- Group exercise classes
- Lap pool and relaxation pool
- Dry sauna and steam room
- Yoga studio

Some salespeople I work with mix up features with benefits. Benefits are the improvements that the product delivers. Features are the different areas of functionality included with the product. If you sold cars, the car is the product. But the features of the car are cruise control, navigation system, anti-lock brakes, sunroof, etc.

Here is another example to show the difference between features and benefits. If you go back to the health and fitness club example, the features are very easy to see as those are treadmills, weights, and classes. A customer does not purchase treadmills; they purchase a membership to the facility, and one feature is a room filled with treadmills. The treadmill is also not an improvement, so it is not a benefit. An improvement that the customer can see by using the treadmill is that he or she might become healthier. With that, the product is the health club membership, one of the features is treadmills, and a benefit is becoming healthier.

PRODUCT GROUPS AND PACKAGES

Next, it may make sense to brainstorm different groupings for your products and services. Here are some groupings for the health and fitness club example:

- Health and fitness club
- Membership and Personal Training Package
- Family Membership Package
- Three months of personal training

The reason you may want to do this extra step is that you may want to create a sales message that includes multiple products or services. One grouping in particular that you might want to put down and create a sales message for is an "everything" product group that includes everything that you sell. If you can create some sort of label, umbrella, or category that can be used to include everything that you sell, you could use that to create a broad sales message that can be used for most prospects and this is often a good first sales message to create.

Pick a Product for Your Sales Message

Once you have brainstormed a list of what you sell, take a step back and pick a product, feature, or grouping that you would like to create your sales message around. If you fully adopt the SMART Sales System, you will likely create more than one sales message, but we believe in a crawl-walk-run approach, and your crawl step would be to create one sales message. As just mentioned, your "everything" product is often a good product for your first sales message and for the crawl phase as it creates a broad sales message that you can use for most prospects and conversations.

Once you feel like you have made progress with your adoption of the SMART Sales System and are ready to move to the walk phase, you can come back and create sales messages that are more focused on the individual products you sell. What this will allow you to do is have a broad message that you can use when starting conversations, and then have more product-specific messages that you can either transition to while talking with a prospect, or to use for different outbound sales and marketing campaigns.

29

When you are ready to go to the next level and advance to your run phase, you can create additional sales messages that are tailored to different audiences that you sell to and we will talk more about that in the next chapter.

Identify How Your Product Differs

For the product that you selected for your sales message, try to think about how it differs from your competition. If your product is different and better in some way, you should try to include this in your sales message. For example, if you sell a software application and your competitor's system will require the customer to pay thousands of dollars for consultants to set it up and your system is set up automatically, this is a key area of differentiation and this needs to be in your sales message.

> *We differ from our competitors in that you can set up our system without having to pay thousands of dollars to hire consultants.*

Your product might be different in some very compelling ways, and it can be easy to forget to bring those up when talking with prospects. With that, our goal here is to identify ways your product is different and then get that into your sales message to make sure you remember to share these important details.

Here are some examples of differentiation to help you to get ideas when thinking about your product:

- *Our system is the only platform that includes a video option.*
- *Our services are on a contingency model, and you are only charged when we find savings.*
- *Our platform offers support for over twenty-five different languages.*
- *We provide real-time data compared to other systems that have a one to two-hour delay.*

For some salespeople, it will be very easy to think of two or three areas of differentiation. For others, this may be difficult, especially if what they sell is a "me too" product and very similar to what the competitors are selling. If this is the case, no big deal—you can either skip this step or you may be able to find ways that you are different outside of the actual product being sold. For example, your product might be the same, but your customer service is better in that your customers actually talk to a human when calling your support phone number. Or your pricing and the way you package your products is different from your competitors. These are definitely things that you can mention when trying to explain how you are better than the competition.

Identify Any Company Bragging Points

If there are any noteworthy or bragging points about your company, try to include those in your sales message. Here are some examples of categories that you might get some ideas from:

- Years in business - *Been in business for thirty years*
- Number of customers - *Have worked with over twenty thousand clients*
- Size of the company - *We have over ten thousand advisors on staff*
- Countries you operate in - *We have offices in over sixty countries*
- Awards you have won - *Capstone Innovation Award for the past two years*
- Significant accomplishments - *Have over one thousand patents on file*
- Financial strength of your company - *We have over $1 billion in cash reserves*
- Ownership details - *Woman-owned, veteran-owned, private, publicly traded, etc.*

This step is optional as there may be nothing really noteworthy about your company, and that is completely OK. But if you have won awards for customer service for three out of the past five years, that is really impressive and something that should be in your sales message.

CHAPTER 5

Target

Product > Target

The next step in the process is to identify the target buyer type for your sales message. This is essentially the type of buyer you will be pursuing and talking to when you are using your sales message. When you are first getting started, this should be quick and easy as you can simply use one of these broad target buyers:

- Businesses
- Small businesses
- Business owners
- Small business owners
- Executives
- People
- Individuals

Using one of these broad target buyer types will allow you to move on to the next step in the process which is outlined in the next chapter. You can either grab a broad label and move on to the next step, or you can follow some of the steps explained in the remainder of this chapter and get more specific with the type of target buyer that you build your message around.

Creating Buyer Persona Focused Sales Messages

If you get more specific with the target buyer type, you can create sales messages that are tailored to the different buyer personas that you sell to, and this can help you to speak the buyer's language when selling. In a very competitive world, this extra step could be the difference that helps you to get the prospect's attention and win the business.

For example, if you sell a software application to large corporations and you can sell to both directors of finance and also directors of IT, the two different departments and managers have different interests and pain points. With that, if you take the extra step to have a unique sales message for these different buyers, you can not only improve your odds of hitting the right hot buttons, but you will also stand to make a better impression by appearing more sophisticated. Both of these factors could directly impact your ability to get into the account and ultimately improve your sales in the long term.

Brainstorming Buyer Types

In order to figure out which target buyer types to create sales messages for, start with simply brainstorming the different buyers that you cross paths with during your sales prospecting efforts. To help you with that, here are some categories and examples of buyers.

SIZE

You may want to think about the size of different buyers that you deal with in terms of revenue or employee count.

- Revenue between $1 million and $10 million
- Employee count between one thousand and ten thousand
- Small businesses
- Multinational corporations

The reason you might want to consider size when creating your messaging is that a small business owner might have very different interests and pain points than a large corporation.

INDUSTRY

You might want to think about some of the different industries that you sell your product to.

- Construction companies
- Retail businesses
- Manufacturers
- Health care providers
- Government agencies (local, state, federal)
- Educational institutions

Having unique sales messages for some of the different industries that you sell to can improve your performance. This is not only because industries can have different interests and pain points, but they also may have their own terminology, and you could include industry specific language into your sales message. This extra step is where you literally start speaking the prospect's language and can stand out from the competition.

DEPARTMENT

If you are in B2B sales, you could likely sell your product into different departments of a company, and the departments that you sell into could be the target buyer type.

- Finance
- IT
- Operations
- Human resources

- Sales
- Marketing

As mentioned in a previous example regarding selling to both finance and IT, you can create unique sales messages for the different departments that you sell into, and this can help you tailor your sales message to focus on the department's unique interests and pain points.

TITLE

Each department of a company will have different levels in terms of organizational structure, and you could create unique sales messages for some of the different roles or levels in the organization.

- CXO's
- VP's
- Directors
- Managers

The reason you may want to consider this is that the different levels of an organization could also have different interests and pain points. For example, a C-Level or VP might be more interested in big picture issues and business results, where as a front-line manager might be more concerned about day-to-day operational details and issues. Because of this, you could have a message that focuses more on business improvements and challenges for prospects who are higher in the organization and have a different message for lower level managers that focuses more on technical improvements and challenges.

SALES STAGE

One extra area that you may want to think about is that you could use a different message for prospects who are at different stages of your sales process.

- Cold prospects
- Referred prospects
- Inbound leads
- Qualified prospects
- Current customers
- Past customers

An example of why this might be worth some consideration is that your sales message for a cold prospect will likely be completely different from what you say to an existing customer who you are trying to upsell or cross-sell.

Campaign Coordinates

If you create a list of buyer types that you sell to, you can combine that with your list of products to create a sales planning tool that we call your campaign coordinates. To create this tool, put your products vertically in one column on the left side and your buyer types in one row across the top to create a matrix that looks something like this:

	Type			Size			Industry			Department			Title			Sales Stage		
	Individuals	Families	Businesses	Small businesses	Corporations	Over 10K employees	Construction	Retail	Manufacturing	Finance	IT	Operations	CEOs	VPs	Directors	Suspect	Current customers	Past Customers
Products and Services																		
gym membership																		
personal training																		
vitamins and supplements																		
nutrition consulting																		
Features																		
free weights and machines																		
treadmills, exercise bikes, elliptical machines																		
group exercise classes																		
lap pool and relaxation pool																		
dry sauna and steam room																		
yoga studio and pilates																		
Product Groups and Packages																		
health and fitness club																		
Membership and Personal Training Package																		
Family Membership Package																		
3 months of personal training																		

This tool creates all of the different combinations of what you sell and who you sell to, and each intersection point is a potential sales message or campaign that you could create. Similar to how longitude and latitude lines create coordinates that you can plot on a map when determining where to go, this creates coordinates you can plot to determine where you want your sales strategy to go.

KNOW WHERE YOU ARE GOING IN ORDER TO GET THERE

Think if we were going to plan a road trip with the hope of seeing some interesting stuff. If you just drive without a target destination, the odds that you achieve your goal of seeing interesting stuff will be much lower than if you plot out the different destinations on the map. In a similar way, you can sell without a plan and just try to sell to everybody and make up your message as you go. But if you have a plan for what you want to sell, who you want to sell to, and what you will say to them, you greatly improve your odds of achieving what you want to do.

HOW TO MAP OUT YOUR CAMPAIGN COORDINATES

The best way to use this tool is to look at the combinations of products and target buyer types and identify situations that you find yourself in frequently. In other words, is there a buyer type that you talk to a lot and can line up with a product that you want to sell? If so, put a checkmark in that box as it might be good for you to create a sales message or campaign for that particular combination. You might also want to look for any combinations that are opportunistic where one of your products fits really well with a particular type of buyer. For example, if there was a change or recent event in an industry that would make businesses need one of your products, you might want to mark that combination and plan to create a sales message or campaign for that particular combination.

On your first pass at this exercise, you might end up with a handful of combinations marked. From there, you can prioritize the combinations to create a plan or order that will make sense for how to create the different sales messages and campaigns.

CHAPTER 6

Value

Product > Target > Value

The next step in the process to create your sales message is to brainstorm the value that your product helps the target buyer type to realize.

What Is Value?

When we use the term "value," we are referring to the benefits and improvements that the prospect is likely to see when he or she uses your product. If we go back to the health and fitness club example, when someone purchases a membership and uses the treadmills, weights, classes, and personal training, that person is likely to see some of these improvements:

- Become healthier
- Decrease stress
- Feel better
- Become more confident

These are all value points that are provided by the product and its features, and by creating a sales message that focuses more on these, you will improve your ability to grab the prospect's attention, build interest, and generate leads.

Three Types of Value

We break the concept of value into three levels or categories:

1. TECHNICAL VALUE

These are the benefits and improvements that your product can deliver that are more technical or at a functional level and can help in areas like processes, systems, and people. Here are some examples of areas where these can be seen:

- Automate manual tasks
- Make something work better
- Decrease the amount of time or effort required to do something
- Make something easier
- Increase visibility or access to information
- Improve communications or connectivity
- Improve the performance of systems, processes, or people
- Improve the reliability of systems, processes, or people

2. BUSINESS VALUE

These are benefits or improvements that your product can deliver that are at a business level, and here are some examples of the areas where these can be seen:

- Increase revenue
- Market share growth
- Improve close rate
- Improve conversion rate
- Decrease cost of goods sold
- Decrease inventory costs
- Decrease labor costs
- Increase profitability
- Decrease risk

- Improve decision-making
- Decrease product delivery time
- Improve the delivery of services
- Improve product quality
- Improve customer satisfaction
- Increase customer retention

The technical value that your product delivers will usually lead to some of these business improvements. For example, if your product automates a manual process (technical value), this will likely lead to a business improvement of a decrease in labor cost. With this relationship between technical and business value, if you have a list of technical improvements that your product provides, you can use that list to develop a correlated set of business benefits by trying to think about how each technical improvement might lead to increased revenue, decreased costs, saved time, etc.

3. PERSONAL VALUE

These are benefits and improvements that your product can deliver that are at a personal level for the prospect, and here are some examples of areas where these can be seen:

- Increase personal income
- Decrease personal expenses
- Increase bonuses or commissions
- Create opportunities for career advancement
- Increase recognition for performance
- Decrease workload
- Decrease stress level
- Increase level of happiness
- Improve work/life balance
- Improve personal relationships

Both technical improvements and business improvements can often lead to personal improvements. For example, if your product helps a manager to spend less time performing manual tasks at work, this might help her to leave work earlier in the day and improve her work/life balance.

Another Option: Keep It Simple

You might read about the three levels of value and start to get a headache and wonder if we are making it more complicated than it needs to be. Breaking things down into these three levels will help you think of improvements that you might have missed and not thought of otherwise. But if this makes things too cumbersome for you, you can certainly ignore the three levels and just brainstorm the improvements your product offers and don't worry about the different categories of technical, business, and personal.

Value Brainstorming Questions

You might already have some thoughts on the benefits that your product offers. Whether that is the case or not, below are some questions that you can go through when trying to think about the different ways that your product can help.

TECHNICAL VALUE

Does [Your Product] help [Target Buyer Type] to:

- Improve any processes? How?
- Make anything work better? How?
- Make anything easier? How?
- Save time? How?
- Improve visibility or access to information? How?
- Improve communications or connectivity? How?
- Make anything more reliable? How?
- Reduce the effort, energy, or manpower needed to do something? How?
- Automate anything? How?

BUSINESS VALUE

Does [Your Product] help [Target Buyer Type] to:

- Decrease costs? How?
- Increase revenue? How?
- Increase profitability? How?
- Improve decision-making? How?
- Decrease risk? How?
- Improve the quality of their products or services? How?
- Improve customer satisfaction? How?

PERSONAL VALUE

Does [Your Product] help [Target Buyer Type] to:

- Increase personal income? How?
- Decrease personal expenses? How?
- Increase the potential for a promotion? How?
- Increase the potential for job performance recognition? How?
- Improve work/life balance? How?
- Decrease stress? How?
- Improve happiness? How?
- Be more comfortable? How?
- Improve job security? How?
- Improve the workplace atmosphere? How?

Moving to the Next Step

After you brainstorm the different improvements that your product offers, you can move on to the next step of the process and chapter in this book where you will brainstorm the pain points that your product helps to resolve. At a minimum, you want to have three value points before moving on as the next step in the process will build off of what you created here.

CHAPTER 7

Pain

Product > Target > Value > Pain

The next step is to identify the pain points and problems that your product helps your customers to resolve, minimize, or avoid.

What Is Pain?

When we refer to pain, we are talking about an area for the prospect that is not working well or could be working better. If we go back to the health and fitness club example, there are certain pain points that would motivate prospects to purchase this product:

- Don't currently have a healthy lifestyle
- Concerned about health issues
- Don't feel good
- Don't feel confident about how they look

If salespeople focus their sales message more on the pain points they help with, they can not only improve their ability to identify if the prospect is a good fit for what they sell, but they will also improve their ability to build interest and motivate the prospect to move forward.

Three Types of Pain

In the exact same way that we broke value into three levels or categories, we do the same for the pain points that you can help with.

1. TECHNICAL PAIN

These are the pain points that your product can resolve that are more technical or at a functional level and can help with areas like processes, systems, and people. Here are some examples of areas where these can be seen:

- Tasks are manual and time-consuming
- Things are not working well
- It takes a lot of time or effort to do something
- Current processes are difficult
- It is difficult to see what is going on and access information
- Connectivity or communicating is difficult
- Performance of systems, processes, or people is not what it needs to be
- Reliability of systems, processes, or people is not what it needs to be

2. BUSINESS PAIN

These are the pain points that your product can resolve that are at a business level, and here are some examples of the areas where these can be seen:

- Difficult to find ways to increase revenue
- Difficult to grow market share
- Difficult to close sales and leads
- Conversion rates are not what they need to be
- Decision-making process is slow and not as good as it needs to be
- Difficult to increase profitability
- High cost of goods sold
- High inventory costs

- High labor costs
- Long product delivery time
- Poor product or service quality
- Customer satisfaction is not what it needs to be
- Customer retention is not what it needs to be

In the same way that technical value can lead to business value, technical pain can lead to business pain. For example, if a process is manual and time-consuming, that will likely be causing labor costs to be higher than they should be. With this relationship, if you brainstorm a good list of technical pain points that your product fixes, you can use that list to develop a correlated list of business pain points. In other words, you can look at each technical pain point and try to identify if that problem will lead to decreased revenue, increased costs, poor customer experience, etc.

3. PERSONAL PAIN

These are the pain points that your product can resolve at a personal level, and here are some examples of the areas where these can be seen:

- Not enough income
- Lack of financial strength
- Not making enough bonuses or commissions
- Need to get promoted or advance career
- Not getting enough recognition
- Working too much or too much of a workload
- Job is extremely stressful and chaotic
- Not a good work/life balance
- Not happy

Both technical pain and business pain can often lead to personal pain. For example, if a process is very time-consuming, this might make a manager have to work late in order to make sure the process is complete, and this could prevent him from getting home to have dinner with his family, creating an unhealthy work/life balance.

Brainstorming the Pain Your Product Resolves

You may be able to think of a few pain points that your product resolves without much thought. That is great; put those down in your notes. But put that to the side and go back to the value points that you identified in the previous step as you can use those to brainstorm the pain points your product resolves.

Each value point will usually have an opposing pain point. In other words, for each improvement that you make, there is usually a problem that is resolved. For example, if you sell a pill that helps someone to sleep better at night (technical value), this solves the problem of tossing and turning at night (technical pain). With this inverse relationship, we can look at each value point and try to identify the opposite of the improvement or what problem is resolved. If you have trouble figuring out what the opposite of a particular improvement is, you can ask these questions:

- If my product is providing this improvement to a customer and I take it away, what problem will start happening?
- If someone does not have this improvement, what will be more difficult to do?
- If someone does not have this improvement, what problems or concerns could exist?

For example, if you sell something that automates a manual and time-consuming process (technical value), you can look at that and assume that some of these pain points might exist without your product being used:

- It takes a lot of time and labor to complete the process (technical pain point)
- The process can sometimes be prone to error due to the human element (technical pain point)
- Labor costs are higher than what they need to be (business pain point)
- The manager has to work late nights to make sure the process is completed (personal pain point)

If you go through your list of value points one at a time and try to come up with at least one pain point for each value point, you should end up with a good list of pain points that your product can help to resolve, minimize, or avoid. But if that does not work for you, here is a list of brainstorming questions similar to those on the value brainstorming step.

TECHNICAL PAIN

If your customer does not have [insert improvement]:

- Will anything be more difficult or not work as well? What?
- Will anything be more time-consuming? What?
- Will there be less visibility in anyway? How?
- Will communications or connectivity be difficult? How?
- Will anything be less reliable? What?
- Will anything require more effort, energy, or manpower? What?

BUSINESS PAIN

If your customer does not have [insert improvement]:

- Will any costs be higher? How?
- Will revenue be lower? How?
- Will profitability be lower? How?
- Will decision-making be more difficult? How?
- Will the level of risk be higher in any areas? How?
- Will the quality of their services or products be lower? How?
- Will their level of customer satisfaction be lower? How?

PERSONAL PAIN

If your customer does not have [insert improvement]:

- Will their personal income be less? How?
- Will their personal expenses be higher? How?
- Will it be less likely for job performance recognition? How?
- Will it be more difficult to maintain a good work/life balance? How?
- Will anything be more stressful? How?
- Will it be more difficult to be happy? How?
- Will life or work be more uncomfortable? How?
- Will there be less job security? How?
- Will the workplace atmosphere be worse? How?

Moving to the Next Step

After you brainstorm the different pain points that your product resolves, you can move on to the next step of the process and chapter, which is where we will discuss composing questions that you can ask to determine if the prospect has any of the pain points that you can help with. At a minimum, you want to have three pain points created from what we discussed in this chapter before moving on to the next step in the process.

CHAPTER 8

Pain Questions

Product > Target > Value > Pain > Pain Questions

The next step is to create pain questions that probe for the pain points that your product helps to resolve, minimize, or avoid.

Finding the Prospect's Pain Isn't Always Easy

Before we talk about developing questions that uncover the prospect's pain, we need to discuss a couple of challenges that you have to be prepared for.

LATENT PAIN

It is important to keep in mind that your prospect could be completely unaware of their pain or problems. For example, someone could drive a car that has a leak in the gas tank and be completely unaware that there is anything wrong because the car can appear to operate without any disruptions or problems. If you were to ask this person if he or she has any issues or even if there is a gas leak, the driver might say no because he or she is completely unaware that the problem exists. This is an example of latent pain, and this is where the prospect is unaware that the pain or problems exist.

STATE OF DENIAL

Another situation that you can encounter is where the prospect might be aware that he or she has pain but there is a state of denial with a response that everything is good. This is similar to when a coach asks an athlete how he or she feels after getting hurt in a game. The athlete may have pain but his or her primary desire is to get back in the game, and as a result, the quick answer may often be "I'm fine." Similar to how an athlete wants to get back in the game and denies having any pain, a prospect may deny having pain in order to get back to work and off a call with a salesperson.

Creating Your Pain-Probing Questions

For each pain point that you came up with in the last step, you can create one or two questions you can ask the prospect to get an idea if he or she has any concerns or problems in that particular area. For example, if you sell something that helps someone to sleep better (technical value) and that solves the problem of tossing and turning at night (technical pain), then good questions to ask the prospect are:

- *How do you feel about the quality of sleep you get every night?*
- *How often do you have trouble sleeping at night?*
- *How happy are you with your level of energy during the day?*

Not only do these questions do a good job of figuring out how well the prospect fits with the product being sold, they are also very conversational, engaging, and consultative and will minimize how much you sound like a salesperson who is trying to sell something.

While that connection between pain points and pain questions is easy to see, it can still sometimes seem unclear what questions to ask. To help with that, here are some tips to help you with composing your pain questions.

TRY TO USE OPEN-ENDED QUESTIONS

Try to avoid sticking a "Do you have..." in front of the pain point to create a pain-probing question. For example:

Technical Pain: Trouble sleeping at night.

Pain Question: *Do you have trouble sleeping at night?*

The problem with that question is that this creates a closed-ended question in that it can be answered with a simple "yes" or "no." Open-ended questions that can't be answered with a "yes" or "no" are better in that they will usually get more information out of the prospect and get him or her talking more and more engaged in the conversation.

"HOW DO YOU FEEL ABOUT..." QUESTIONS

You can create pain questions that ask the prospect about his or her feelings regarding the area of the pain point instead of asking if the prospect has the pain point. For example, if you solve the problem that it takes a lot of time to train new salespeople, you could ask any of these questions:

- *How do you feel about the amount of time that it takes to train new salespeople?*
- *How concerned are you about the amount of time that it takes to train new salespeople?*
- *Have you ever been concerned about the amount of time that it takes to train new salespeople?*
- *How happy are you with the amount of time that it takes to train new salespeople?*

The logic is that this makes the question softer, less specific, and broader, and this can work better in situations where the prospect is not aware of pain or is in a state of denial.

"HOW IMPORTANT IS IT FOR YOU..." QUESTIONS

Another way to phrase your pain questions is to ask about the level of priority or importance. This is an approach where you are almost assuming that the prospect has the pain, and you are inquiring about how the issue ranks on his or her list of priorities or concerns.

For example, if you help businesses to increase their website traffic, you can assume that every prospect wants to increase website traffic. With that, to ask prospects "Do you need more website traffic?" or "How do you feel about your traffic?" might not be the optimum way to probe for pain because you can assume that they want more traffic.

A better way to go is to ask about the priority or importance of increasing website traffic, and here are a couple examples of that:

- *How much of a priority is it for you to find new ways to increase your website traffic?*
- *How important is it for you to find new ways to increase your website traffic?*

"WHEN WAS THE LAST TIME YOU..." QUESTIONS

One way you can ask about a pain point is by inquiring about the past. For example, if your product finds errors in vendor invoicing, instead of asking if they have errors in their invoices, you could inquiry about the past by asking any of these questions:

- *How often have you experienced errors in your invoices?*
- *When was the last time you analyzed your invoices for errors?*
- *How often do you reconcile your vendor invoices?*

YES/NO QUESTIONS

Earlier I mentioned that you should try to make your questions open-ended where they can't be answered with a "yes" or "no." But sometimes it is good to ask very direct yes/no questions, and this is when having a very precise yes/no answer is valuable information for you. Here are some examples of closed-ended questions that might lead to valuable information:

- *Do you currently have a system in place for error scanning?*
- *Have you ever had trouble synchronizing data across systems?*
- *Is your process for transferring sales data manual?*

DON'T BE TOO INVASIVE

Be cautious of asking questions that are too invasive in terms of asking for information that the prospect might not be open to sharing with you. For example, if you solve a pain point around fines or compliance, to ask prospects about fines they have had to pay or if they are currently compliant would be too invasive to ask when first talking with them. You can resolve that by using the "How do you feel about..." structure with something like this:

- *How do you feel about your ability to meet all of the different compliance requirements?*
- *How concerned are you about getting fined for compliance issues?*

Or you could use the "How important is it for you..." structure with something like this:

- *How important is it for you to improve your ability to stay compliant?*
- *How much of a priority is it for you to decrease having to pay fines for compliance issues?*

Moving to the Next Step

After you compose a few pain questions that probe to see if your prospect has some of the problems or concerns that your product resolves, you can move on to the next step of the process and chapter, where we will discuss creating a short example of a customer you have helped. At a minimum, you want to have three pain questions created from what we discussed in this chapter before moving on to the next step in the process.

CHAPTER 9

Name-Drop

Product > Target > Value > Pain > Pain Questions > Name-Drop

The next step in the process is to create a short story of a customer that your product has helped. We call this short story a name-drop example, and we will provide a process that you can use to create your name-drop example in this chapter.

> ***Note:*** *This step is optional. If you do not have a good customer example to share, that is not a problem at all as you can skip this step and still have a very good sales message.*

Creating Your Customer Example

Here are four steps to go through to gather the details we need to create your name-drop example.

1. PICK A CUSTOMER

The first step is to pick a current or past customer who would be a good example to share with prospects. If possible, try to pick a customer who is similar to the target buyer type that you selected for your sales message.

Target > Name-Drop

There could be a scenario where you have an example to share but don't have approval or feel comfortable sharing the actual name. You can certainly follow this process and use a descriptive label for the customer instead of sharing an actual name.

2. IDENTIFY THE PRODUCT THAT YOU SOLD TO THE NAME-DROP CUSTOMER

For this step, simply identify the product or service you provided to the name-drop customer.

Target > Name-Drop > Product

In most cases, this would be the product that you selected for the sales message.

3. IDENTIFY THE TECHNICAL IMPROVEMENT THE CUSTOMER REALIZED

Identify a technical improvement that your product created for the name-drop customer. This could be a short sentence that shares how you helped to make things work better from a process, system, or people standpoint.

Target > Name-Drop > Product > Technical Value

If you need some help getting ideas on how you might have helped the name-drop customer, go back to the brainstorming questions in Chapter 6 and the value points that you came up with.

4. IDENTIFY THE BUSINESS IMPROVEMENT THE CUSTOMER REALIZED

The last step is to identify a business improvement that was created by the technical improvement your product delivered. This could be a short sentence that shares how you helped to improve revenue, costs, delivery of services, etc.

Target > Name-Drop > Product > Technical Value > Business Value

Again, if you need more help getting ideas for how you helped the name-drop customer, go back to the brainstorming questions in Chapter 6 and the value points that you came up with.

Creating Your Name-Drop Example

If you answer those four simple questions, you can create a very powerful name-drop blurb by simply plugging those answers into this template:

- *We worked with [insert customer name] and helped them to [insert technical improvement].*
- *We were able to do this by providing our [insert the product or service you sold].*
- *This ultimately helped them to [insert business improvement].*

Once you have a name-drop blurb, you can put that in a lot of different places in your sales scripts, email templates, and voicemail messages. We will show you that in the next few chapters in this book.

CHAPTER 10

Building Blocks

We can take all of the points that you created in the previous steps to create what we call "building blocks," and those are outlined below. This basically takes all of the individual points and puts them together into blocks for different topics and talk tracks that you can discuss with prospects. Once you have these building blocks filled in with your sales message, we can use them to easily build a lot of different scripts, emails, and sales tools, and we will do that in Section 2 of this book.

Product

We provide [Product Name] and that includes:

- *Feature 1*
- *Feature 2*
- *Feature 3*

Benefits
Our [Product Name] can help [Target Buyer Type] to:

- *Value Point 1*
- *Value Point 2*
- *Value Point 3*

Differentiation

Some ways that we differ from other options out there are:

- *Differentiation 1*
- *Differentiation 2*
- *Differentiation 3*

Impact of Doing Nothing

Some things to be concerned about when not doing anything in this area are:

- *Pain Point 1*
- *Pain Point 2*
- *Pain Point 3*

Company Bragging Points

Other key details about us are:

- *Company Fact 1*
- *Company Fact 2*
- *Company Fact 3*

Value Points

We help [Target Buyer Type] to:

- *Value Point 1*
- *Value Point 2*
- *Value Point 3*

Pain Points

When I talk with other [Target Buyer Type], they often have challenges with:

- *Pain Point 1*
- *Pain Point 2*
- *Pain Point 3*

Are you concerned about any of those areas?

Pain Questions

If I could ask you real quick:

- *Pain Question 1*
- *Pain Question 2*
- *Pain Question 3*

Name-Drop

- *We worked with [Customer Name] and helped them to [Technical Improvement].*
- *We were able to do this by providing our [Product Name].*
- *This ultimately helped them to [Business Improvement].*

Current Environment Questions

- *Who are you currently using today?*
- *How long have you been with them?*

- *How is everything going?*
- *What are some things you like about what they provide?*
- *What are some things that you think could be better?*
- *If you could change one thing about their product/service, what would it be?*
- *When was the last time you considered other options in this area?*
- *(Sizing Question) How many _____ do you currently have?*
- *Are you the right person to discuss this area with?*

Qualifying Questions

Need vs. Want
- *What motivated you to look at us (brought you to us)?*
- *Do you mind if I ask why you took time out of your schedule to meet with us?*
- *What improvements could you see if you make this purchase?*
- *What will happen if you do not purchase something?*
- *Is there a date when this purchase needs to be made?*
- *What happens if the purchase is not made by that date?*
- *What is the time frame that the project needs to work along?*

Funding Availability
- *What is the budgetary range that you need this purchase to stay within?*
- *Is there a budget approved for this project?*
- *Have the funds been allocated to this purchase?*
- *What budget (department) will this purchase be made under?*
- *Are there other purchases that this funding may end up being used for?*
- *How does the project fit with other initiatives from a priority standpoint?*

Decision Authority
- *What is the decision-making process?*
- *What parties will be involved in making the decision?*
- *What are the key factors that a decision will be based on?*

- *What functional areas (departments) will be impacted by the purchase?*
- *Is there a committee that this type of purchase has to go through?*
- *Who is the ultimate decision maker?*
- *Who is the person that will need to sign the agreement/contract?*

Level of Competition

- *What other options are you considering?*
- *How far along are you in discussions with them?*
- *How do you feel about your other options?*
- *What do you like about them?*
- *What do you not like about them?*
- *How do they compare with what we have to offer?*
- *Is there a reason why you would choose us over them?*
- *If you had to make a decision today, which way would you lean?*

Sales Takeaway

- *I do not know if you need what we provide.*
- *I do not know if you are a good fit with what we do.*
- *I do not know if we can help you in the same way that we have helped others.*
- *I do not know if you are interested in those improvements.*
- *I do not know if you are concerned about those areas.*
- *I do not know if you are the right person to speak with.*
- *I do not know if it makes sense for us to talk.*
- *Maybe this is not the right time for you to look at this purchase.*
- *Maybe we are not the right product for you.*
- *Maybe this is more than you need right now.*

Cold Call Close

But I have called you out of the blue, and I am not sure if this is the best time to discuss this.

Are you interested in discussing this a little more?

Are you available for a brief 15 to 20 minute meeting where I can share some examples of how we have helped other [Target Buyer Type] to:

- *Value Point 1*
- *Value Point 2*
- *Value Point 3*

Or are you available to continue talking about this now?

Closing Questions

Trial Closing
- *What do you think about what you have seen so far?*
- *How do you think this fits with what you are needing?*
- *How would that feature help you?*
- *Is this something you could see your organization using?*
- *Are we heading in the right direction?*
- *Is this what you were expecting to see?*

Soft Closing
- *What would you like to do next?*
- *What direction do you want to go from here?*
- *Do you want to continue talking about this?*

- *When would you like to talk again?*
- *What does the path forward look like?*

Hard Closing

- *Are you ready to move forward to the next step in the process?*
- *What would you need to be able to make a commitment to move forward?*
- *If you had everything that you are asking for, are you prepared to move forward?*
- *When are you going to make your final decision?*
- *(If delaying the decision for a period of time) OK, but do you mind if I ask if there will be a change or something different at that time that will make it a better time to look at moving forward?*
- *Is there anything that is preventing you from being able to move forward with this purchase?*

Meeting Warm-Up Questions

- *How is your day going so far?*
- *[Ask a question regarding the weather, sports, recent current event, etc.]*
- *How long have you been working here?*
- *What did you do before this?*
- *Where are you from?*
- *What do you like most about what you do?*
- *I know why I wanted to meet with you. Is there anything that motivated you to want to meet with me?*
- *[Share agenda for meeting] Does that match up with your expectations for this meeting?*
- *Is there anything in particular that you are hoping to get out of this meeting?*
- *Do you have a hard stop for this meeting?*

Networking Questions

- *How is your day going so far?*
- *What do you do?*
- *How long have you been doing that?*
- *What did you do before?*
- *What do you like most about what you do?*
- *Is there something that motivated you to get into that type of work?*
- *Where are you from?*
- *What brought you to this event?*
- *Have you found this to be a productive event for you?*
- *Are there any other networking events that you recommend?*
- *How can I help you to be successful?*
- *What does a good prospect look like for you?*
- *What is the best way to refer business to you?*
- *What is the best way to stay in touch?*
- *What is the best way to work together?*

LEVEL 2—SALES TOOLS

CHAPTER 11

Call Scripts

We can use the sales message and building blocks created in the previous section of this book to create a number of different call scripts. These scripts basically mix and match all of the different building blocks to give you different options for how you can try to organize your calls. We will talk more about cold calling and how to use these scripts in Chapter 17.

Cold Call Script – Value Points Intro

This is a cold call script that uses your value proposition to open the call and then drives toward trying to ask some of your pain questions.

Introduction

Hello, [Contact's Name]. This is [Your Name] with [Your Company]. Have I caught you in the middle of anything?

Value Points

Great. The reason for my call is that we help [Target Buyer Type] to:

- *Value Point 1*
- *Value Point 2*
- *Value Point 3*

Sales Takeaway

I actually don't know if those are areas that you want to improve and that is why I wanted to call you with a question or two.

Pain Questions

If I could ask you real quick:

- *Pain Question 1*
- *Pain Question 2*
- *Pain Question 3*

Current Environment Questions

- *Who are you currently using today?*
- *How long have you been with them?*
- *How is everything going?*
- *What are some things you like about what they provide?*
- *What are some things that you think could be better?*
- *If you could change one thing about their product/service, what would it be?*
- *When was the last time you considered other options in this area?*
- *(Sizing Question) How many _____ do you currently have?*
- *Are you the right person to discuss this area with?*

Pain Points

When I talk with other [Target Buyer Type], they often have challenges with:

- *Pain Point 1*
- *Pain Point 2*
- *Pain Point 3*

Are you concerned about any of those areas?

Product

We provide [Product Name] and that includes:

- *Feature 1*
- *Feature 2*
- *Feature 3*

Benefits

Our [Product Name] can help [Target Buyer Type] to:

- *Value Point 1*
- *Value Point 2*
- *Value Point 3*

Differentiation

Some ways that we differ from other options out there are:

- *Differentiation 1*
- *Differentiation 2*
- *Differentiation 3*

Impact of Doing Nothing

Some things to be concerned about when not doing anything in this area are:

- *Pain Point 1*
- *Pain Point 2*
- *Pain Point 3*

Company Bragging Points

Other key details about us are:

- *Company Fact 1*
- *Company Fact 2*
- *Company Fact 3*

Name-Drop

- *We worked with [Customer Name] and helped them to [Technical Improvement].*

- *We were able to do this by providing our [Product Name].*
- *This ultimately helped them to [Business Improvement].*

Cold Call Close

But I have called you out of the blue and I am not sure if this is the best time to discuss this.

Are you interested in discussing this a little more?

Are you available for a brief 15 to 20 minute meeting where I can share some examples of how we have helped other [Target Buyer Type] to:

- *Value Point 1*
- *Value Point 2*
- *Value Point 3*

Or are you available to continue talking about this now?

Cold Call Script – Pain Points Intro

This script uses your pain points to open the call. A reason you might want to use this script is if the pain points that your product helps with are very compelling or attention-grabbing.

Introduction

Hello, [Contact's Name]. This is [Your Name] with [Your Company]. Have I caught you in the middle of anything?

Pain Points

Great. The reason for my call is that we work [Target Buyer Type] and help them to solve the challenges of:

- *Pain Point 1*
- *Pain Point 2*
- *Pain Point 3*

Sales Takeaway

I actually don't know if you are concerned about any of those areas and that is why I wanted to call you with a question or two.

Pain Questions

(Standard building block)

Current Environment Questions

(Standard building block)

Product

(Standard building block)

Name-Drop

(Standard building block)

Cold Call Close

(Standard building block)

Cold Call Script – Name-Drop Intro

This script uses your name-drop example to open the call. This might be a good script to use if you have an impressive customer example that you think might do a good job of grabbing the prospect's attention and explain how you can help.

Introduction

> Hello, [Contact's Name]. This is [Your Name] with [Your Company]. Have I caught you in the middle of anything?

Name-Drop

> Great. The reason for my call is that:
>
> - We worked with [Customer Name] and helped them to [Technical Improvement].
> - This ultimately helped them to [insert business improvement].

Sales Takeaway

> I actually don't know if we can help you in the same way or not and that is why I wanted to call you with a question or two.

Pain Questions

(Standard building block)

Current Environment Questions

(Standard building block)

Pain Points

(Standard building block)

Product

(Standard building block)

Cold Call Close

(Standard building block)

Cold Call Script – Product Intro

This is a cold call script that opens the call by talking about the product. We typically suggest that you save product details toward the end of the call, but there may be a situation where it makes more sense to open the call by sharing what you sell, and here is a script for that. We stick your full product building block in the beginning of this script, and it is up to you which of these product details you share as you try to open the call.

Introduction

Hello, [Contact's Name]. This is [Your Name] with [Your Company].
Have I caught you in the middle of anything?

Product

Great. The reason for the call is that we provide [Product Name] and that includes:

- *Feature 1*
- *Feature 2*
- *Feature 3*

Benefits
Our [Product Name] can help [Target Buyer Type] to:

- *Value Point 1*
- *Value Point 2*
- *Value Point 3*

Differentiation
Some ways that we differ from other options out there are:

- *Differentiation 1*
- *Differentiation 2*
- *Differentiation 3*

Impact of Doing Nothing

Some things to be concerned about when not doing anything in this area are:

- *Pain Point 1*
- *Pain Point 2*
- *Pain Point 3*

Company Bragging Points

Other key details about us are:

- *Company Fact 1*
- *Company Fact 2*
- *Company Fact 3*

Sales Takeaway

I actually don't know if you are a good fit with what we provide and that is why I wanted to call you with a question or two.

Pain Questions

(Standard building block)

Current Environment Questions

(Standard building block)

Pain Points

(Standard building block)

Name-Drop

(Standard building block)

Cold Call Close

(Standard building block)

Cold Call Script – Quick Close

This is a cold call script that goes for the close in the early part of the call.

Introduction

> *Hello, [Contact's Name]. This is [Your Name] with [Your Company].*
> *Have I caught you in the middle of anything?*

Cold Call Quick Close

> *Great. What I would like to do is share some examples of how we*
> *have helped other [Target Buyer Type] to:*

- *Value Point 1*
- *Value Point 2*
- *Value Point 3*

> *That is usually a brief 15 to 20 minute conversation. Is that something*
> *that we can put on your calendar or are you available to continue*
> *talking about this now?*

Pain Questions
(Standard building block)

Current Environment Questions
(Standard building block)

Pain Points
(Standard building block)

Product

(Standard building block)

Name-Drop

(Standard building block)

Cold Call Script – Event Follow-Up

This is a cold call script that you could use to call someone who attended an event that you hosted. For example, if someone attended a webinar event that you or your company hosted, you could call him or her after the event with this type of approach.

Introduction

> Hello, [Contact's Name]. This is [Your Name] with [Your Company]. Have I caught you in the middle of anything?

Recap

> Great. The reason for my call is that I see that you attended our [Name of Event] and I just wanted to do my part to follow up with you.

Event Questions

- *Do you have any thoughts on the event?*
- *Was there any information provided that you found helpful?*
- *Is there any information that you need or wanted that you did not get?*
- *Are there any questions you have from the event?*
- *Did you think it was a good use of your time?*
- *What motivated you to sign up and come to the event?*

Pain Questions

(Standard building block)

Current Environment Questions

(Standard building block)

Pain Points

(Standard building block)

Product

(Standard building block)

Name-Drop

(Standard building block)

Cold Call Close

(Standard building block)

Cold Call Script – Website Document Download

This is a cold call script that you could use to call someone who visited your website and downloaded a marketing document. For example, if someone downloaded an ebook or document, you could call him or her with this type of approach.

Introduction

Hello, [Contact's Name]. This is [Your Name] with [Your Company]. Have I caught you in the middle of anything?

Recap

Great. The reason for my call is that I see that you downloaded our [Name of document] and I just wanted to do my part to follow up with you.

Download Questions

- *Did the document provide you with what you were looking for?*
- *Was there anything that you found helpful?*
- *Is there any information that you are still looking for?*
- *Do you mind if I ask what motivated you to come to our site and download the document?*

Pain Questions

(Standard building block)

Current Environment Questions

(Standard building block)

Pain Points

(Standard building block)

Product

(Standard building block)

Name-Drop

(Standard building block)

Cold Call Close

(Standard building block)

Cold Call Script – Customer Check-In and Cross-Sell

This is a cold call script that you could use to call a current customer and create an opportunity to talk about other products you sell.

Introduction

Hello, [Contact's Name]. This is [Your Name] with [Your Company]. Have I caught you in the middle of anything?

Recap

Great. The reason for my call is that I see that you currently use our [Purchased Product] and I just wanted to do my part to check in with you.

Purchased Product Questions

- *How is everything going with [Purchased Product]?*
- *Is there anything that you like about it or find that is working well?*
- *Is there anything that you think could be working better?*
- *Do you mind if I ask what motivated you to purchase [Purchased Product]?*

Pain Questions
(Standard building block)

Current Environment Questions
(Standard building block)

Pain Points

(Standard building block)

Product

(Standard building block)

Name-Drop

(Standard building block)

Cold Call Close

(Standard building block)

CHAPTER 12

Email Templates

We can use your sales message and building blocks to create a number of sales prospecting email messages. We will talk more about email prospecting and how to use these emails in Chapter 18.

Cold Email Messages

These are some cold emails that are designed to be sent to prospects you have not spoken with and who do not know you or your company.

COLD EMAIL – VALUE POINTS

This is an email that focuses on the value you have to offer the prospect.

Subject Line: [Value Point]

Hello [Contact First Name],

The reason for the email is that we help [Target Buyer Type] to:

- Value Point 1
- Value Point 2
- Value Point 3

I don't know if you want to improve those areas and that is why I am reaching out.

Are you available for a brief 15 to 20 minute meeting where I can share some examples of how we have helped other [Target Buyer Type] to [Value Point]?

Best Regards,
[Email Signature]

COLD EMAIL – PAIN POINTS

We can take the previous email and simply change the value building block to the pain points building block and end up with an email like this.

Subject Line: [Pain Point]

Hello [Contact First Name],

The reason for the email is that we help [Target Buyer Type] with the challenges of:

- Pain Point 1
- Pain Point 2
- Pain Point 3

I don't know if you are concerned about any of those areas and that is why I am reaching out.

Are you available for a brief 15 to 20 minute meeting where I can share some examples of how we have helped other [Target Buyer Type] to [Value Point]?

Best Regards,
[Email Signature]

COLD EMAIL – NAME-DROP

We can use the name-drop building block to create an email that looks like this.

Subject Line: [Technical or Business Improvement Realized]

Hello [Contact First Name],

The reason for the email is that we worked with [Customer Name] and helped them to [Technical Improvement].

This ultimately led to them being able to [Business Improvement].

I don't know if we can help you in the same way and that is why I am reaching out.

Are you available for a brief 15 to 20 minute meeting where I can share some examples of how we have helped other [Target Buyer Type] to [Value Point]?

Best Regards,
[Email Signature]

COLD EMAIL – PAIN QUESTIONS

We can use the pain questions building block to create an email that looks like this.

> Subject Line: [Pain Question]
>
> Hello [Contact First Name],
>
> I am trying to determine if we can help you in the same way that have helped our other clients. These are some of the questions that I would ask you to figure that out:
>
> - Pain Question 1
> - Pain Question 2
> - Pain Question 3
>
> Do any of those connect with a challenge or interest that you have?
>
> If so, let's put a few minutes on the calendar to have a brief conversation.
>
> Best Regards,
> [Email Signature]

COLD EMAIL – PRODUCT

This is an email template that explains the product that you have to offer.

> Subject Line: [Product Name]
>
> Hello [Contact First Name],

The reason for the email is that we provide [Product Name] and that includes:

- Feature 1
- Feature 2
- Feature 3

Some ways we differ from other options out there are:

- Differentiation 1
- Differentiation 2
- Differentiation 3

Are you available for a brief 15 to 20 minute meeting where I can share some examples of how we have helped other [Target Buyer Type] to [Value Point]?

Best Regards,
[Email Signature]

THE KEEP ME IN MIND COLD EMAIL – PRODUCT

This is a cold email that you can send to try to coach the prospect to keep you in mind when he or she is ready to purchase or make a change.

Subject Line: Keep us in mind - [Product Name or Area]

Hello [Contact First Name],

Since you are a [Target Buyer Type], you might need or purchase [Product Name or Area] from time-to-time.

We provide [Product Name or Area], so please keep us in mind when you are ready to make a purchase or change.

Some ways that we differ from your other options are:

- Differentiation 1
- Differentiation 2
- Differentiation 3

Let me know if you reach a point where you would like to schedule a brief call to discuss.

Best Regards,
[Email Signature]

LAST ATTEMPT COLD EMAIL – VALUE POINTS

This is a last attempt message that you can send to a prospect that uses your value points.

Subject Line: Checking In

Hello [Contact First Name],

I never heard back from you and I thought I would follow up with you one last time. The reason I am trying to connect with you is that we help [Target Buyer Type] with:

- Value Point 1
- Value Point 2
- Value Point 3

If I don't hear back from you, I will assume you are not interested in those improvements or that you are the not right person to speak with and I will close the file.

If I should be contacting someone else regarding this, any pointing in the right direction would be greatly appreciated.

Best Regards,
[Email Signature]

LAST ATTEMPT COLD EMAIL – PAIN POINTS

This is a last attempt message that you can send to a prospect that uses your pain points.

Subject Line: Checking In

Hello [Contact First Name],

I never heard back from you and I thought I would follow up with you one last time. The reason I am trying to connect with you is that we help [Target Buyer Type] with the challenges of:

- Pain Point 1
- Pain Point 2
- Pain Point 3

If I don't hear back from you, I will assume you are not concerned about those areas or that you are the not right person to speak with and I will close the file.

If I should be contacting someone else regarding this, any pointing in the right direction would be greatly appreciated.

Best Regards,
[Email Signature]

Follow-Up Email Messages

Here are some email messages for common follow-up situations.

SEND YOUR INFO – VALUE POINTS

There are times when you briefly speak with prospects and they ask you to send them your information. Here is an email that uses your value points as the key piece of information that you send to them.

Subject Line: [Value Point]

Hello [Contact First Name],

It was good to briefly speak with you today. As I mentioned, I am with [Your Company] and we help [Target Buyer Type] to:

- Value Point 1
- Value Point 2
- Value Point 3

I don't know if you want to improve those areas and that is why I am reaching out.

Are you available for a brief 15 to 20 minute meeting where I can share some examples of how we have helped other [Target Buyer Type] to [Value Point]?

Best Regards,
[Email Signature]

SEND YOUR INFO – PAIN POINTS

Here is an email that you can send when prospects ask you to send your information that focuses on your pain points as the key piece of information that you send to them.

Subject Line: [Pain Point]

Hello [Contact First Name],

It was good to briefly speak with you today. As I mentioned, I am with [Your Company] and we help [Target Buyer Type] with the challenges of:

- Pain Point 1
- Pain Point 2
- Pain Point 3

I don't know if you are concerned about any of those areas and that is why I am reaching out to you.

Are you available for a brief 15 to 20 minute meeting where I can share some examples of how we have helped other [Target Buyer Type] to [Value Point]?

Best Regards,
[Email Signature]

SEND YOUR INFO – PAIN POINTS, VALUE POINTS, AND PRODUCT

Here is an email that you can send to a prospect who asks for you to send your info that has details about your pain points, value points, and product.

> Subject Line: [Your Company]
>
> Hello [Contact First Name],
>
> It was good to briefly talk with you today. Here is some more information on us and why I am reaching out to you.
>
> We help [Target Buyer Type] with the challenges of:
>
> - Pain Point 1
> - Pain Point 2
> - Pain Point 3
>
> We resolve and mitigate those by driving the following improvements:
>
> - Value Point 1
> - Value Point 2
> - Value Point 3
>
> We do this by providing [Product Name] and that includes:
>
> - Feature 1
> - Feature 2
> - Feature 3
>
> Some ways that we differ from other options out there are:

- Differentiation 1
- Differentiation 2
- Differentiation 3

Are you available for a brief 15 to 20 minute meeting where I can share some examples of how we have helped other [Target Buyer Type] to [Value Point]?

Best Regards,
[Email Signature]

VOICEMAIL FOLLOW-UP EMAIL – VALUE POINTS

This is an email you can send after you leave a voicemail message for the prospect that focuses on your value points.

Subject Line: Following Up My Voicemail - [Your Company]

Hello [Contact First Name],

As I mentioned in a voicemail I just left you, we help [Target Buyer Type] to:

- Value Point 1
- Value Point 2
- Value Point 3

I don't know if you want to improve those areas and that is why I am reaching out.

Are you available for a brief 15 to 20 minute meeting where I can share some examples of how we have helped other [Target Buyer Type] to [Value Point]?

Best Regards,
[Email Signature]

VOICEMAIL FOLLOW-UP EMAIL – PAIN POINTS

This is an email you can send after leaving a sales prospect a voicemail message that focuses on your pain points.

Subject Line: Following Up My Voicemail - [Your Company]

Hello [Contact First Name],

As I mentioned in a voicemail I just left you, we help [Target Buyer Type] with the challenges of:

- Pain Point 1
- Pain Point 2
- Pain Point 3

I don't know if you are concerned about any of those areas and that is why I am reaching out.

Are you available for a brief 15 to 20 minute meeting where I can share some examples of how we have helped other [Target Buyer Type] to [Value Point]?

Best Regards,
[Email Signature]

VOICEMAIL FOLLOW-UP EMAIL – NAME-DROP

This is an email you can send after leaving a sales prospect a voicemail message that focuses on your name-drop example.

Subject Line: Following Up My Voicemail - [Your Company]

Hello [Contact First Name],

As I mentioned in a voicemail I just left you, we worked with [Customer Name] and helped them to [Technical Improvement].

This ultimately led to them being able to [Business Improvement].

I don't know if we can help you in the same way and that is why I am reaching out.

Are you available for a brief 15 to 20 minute meeting where I can share some examples of how we have helped other [Target Buyer Type] to [Value Point]?

Best Regards,
[Email Signature]

VOICEMAIL FOLLOW-UP EMAIL – PRODUCT

This is an email you can send after leaving a sales prospect a voicemail message that focuses on your product.

Subject Line: Following Up My Voicemail - [Your Company]

Hello [Contact First Name],

As I mentioned in a voicemail I just left you, we provide [Product Name] and that includes:

- Feature 1
- Feature 2
- Feature 3

Some ways that we differ from other options out there are:

- Differentiation 1
- Differentiation 2
- Differentiation 3

Are you available for a brief 15 to 20 minute meeting where I can share some examples of how we have helped other [Target Buyer Type] to [Value Point]?

Best Regards,
[Email Signature]

CHECKING BACK IN – VALUE POINTS

This is an email that you can send to follow up with a prospect you have not talked to in a long time that focuses on your value points.

Subject Line: Following back up with you

Hello [Contact First Name],

It has been a little while since we spoke so I thought I would check back in with you.

One reason I thought it might make sense to continue our discussion is that we help [Target Buyer Type] to:

- Value Point 1
- Value Point 2
- Value Point 3

Are those improvements that you are interested in? If so, it might be productive to get back together at some point.

Best Regards,
[Email Signature]

CHECKING BACK IN – PAIN POINTS

This is an email that you can send to follow up with a prospect you have not talked to in a long time.

Subject Line: Following back up with you

Hello [Contact First Name],

It has been a little while since we spoke so I thought I would check back in with you.

One reason I thought it might make sense to continue our discussion is that we help [Target Buyer Type] with the challenges of:

- Pain Point 1
- Pain Point 2
- Pain Point 3

Are those areas you are concerned about? If so, it might be productive to get back together at some point.

Best Regards,
[Email Signature]

NETWORKING FOLLOW-UP EMAIL

This is an email you can send to follow up with someone you met while networking.

Subject Line: Great meeting you!

Hi [Contact First Name],

Great meeting you at [name of event]. I enjoyed our conversation and would like to learn more about what you are doing.

Are you interested in meeting for coffee so that we can continue our conversation?

Best Regards,
[Email Signature]

CHAPTER 13

Voicemail Messages

We can use your sales message and building blocks to create the following voicemail messages. We will talk more about how to incorporate these voicemail messages into your prospecting in Chapter 19 when we talk about voicemail strategy.

VOICEMAIL MESSAGE – VALUE POINTS

This voicemail message focuses on the value that your product offers.

> *Hello [Prospect Name], this is [Your Name] and I am with [Your Company].*
>
> *The reason for my call is that we help [Target Buyer Type] to:*
>
> *(Share 1 to 3 benefits)*
>
> - *Value Point 1*
> - *Value Point 2*
> - *Value Point 3*
>
> *I don't know if you want to improve those areas and that is why I am reaching out.*

I will try you again next week. If you would like to reach me in the meantime, my number is [Your Number].

Again, this is [Your Name] calling from [Your Company], [Your Number Again].

Thank you and I look forward to talking with you soon.

VOICEMAIL MESSAGE – PAIN POINTS

This voicemail message focuses on the problems that your product helps to resolve, minimize, or avoid.

Hello [Prospect Name], this is [Your Name] and I am with [Your Company].

The reason for my call is that we help [Target Buyer Type] with the challenges of:

(Share 1 to 3 pain points)

- *Pain Point 1*
- *Pain Point 2*
- *Pain Point 3*

I don't know if you are concerned about those areas and that is why I am reaching out.

I will try you again next week. If you would like to reach me in the meantime, my number is [Your Number].

Again, this is [Your Name] calling from [Your Company], [Your Number Again].

Thank you and I look forward to talking with you soon.

VOICEMAIL MESSAGE – NAME-DROP

This voicemail message focuses on an example of a customer that you have helped.

Hello [Prospect Name], this is [Your Name] and I am with [Your Company].

The reason for my call is that we worked with [Customer Name] and helped them to [Technical Improvement].

This ultimately led to them being able to [Business Improvement].

I don't know if we can help you in the same way and that is why I am reaching out.

I will try you again next week. If you would like to reach me in the meantime, my number is [Your Number].

Again, this is [Your Name] calling from [Your Company], [Your Number Again].

Thank you and I look forward to talking with you soon.

VOICEMAIL MESSAGE – PRODUCT

This voicemail message focuses on the product that you sell.

Hello [Prospect Name], this is [Your Name] and I am with [Your Company].

The reason for my call is that we provide [Product Name] and that includes:

- *Feature 1*
- *Feature 2*
- *Feature 3*

Some ways that we differ from other options out there are:

- *Differentiation 1*
- *Differentiation 2*
- *Differentiation 3*

I don't know if you are a good fit with what we provide and that is why I am reaching out.

I will try you again next week. If you would like to reach me in the meantime, my number is [Your Number].

Again, this is [Your Name] calling from [Your Company], [Your Number Again].

Thank you and I look forward to talking with you soon.

CHAPTER 14

Objection Responses

We can use your sales message and building blocks to create responses to a lot of the most common sales objections, and those are outlined here. We will talk more about how to use these responses and getting around objections in Chapter 21.

I do not have time right now.

> Oh, I understand. I can be very brief, or I can call you back at another time. Which would work better for you?

> or

> Oh, OK. When is the best time for me to call you back?

What is this in regards to?
Value Points

> The reason for my call is that we help [Target Buyer Type] to:

> - Value Point 1
> - Value Point 2
> - Value Point 3

Is this a sales call?
Value Points

> *The reason for my call is that we help [Target Buyer Type] to:*

- *Value Point 1*
- *Value Point 2*
- *Value Point 3*

I am not interested.
Option 1: Pain Questions

> *I understand. If I could ask you real quick:*

- *Pain Question 1*
- *Pain Question 2*
- *Pain Question 3*

I am not interested.
Option 2: Pain Points

> *I understand. When I talk with other [Target Buyer Type], they often have challenges with:*

- *Pain Point 1*
- *Pain Point 2*
- *Pain Point 3*

> *Are you concerned about any of those areas?*

Just send me your information.
Option 1: Pain Questions

> *I can certainly do that. So that I know what best to send you, can I ask you real quick:*

- *Pain Question 1*
- *Pain Question 2*
- *Pain Question 3*

Just send me your information.
Option 2: Current Environment Questions

> *I can certainly do that. So that I know what best to send you, can I ask you real quick:*

- *Who are you currently using today?*
- *How long have you been with them?*
- *How is everything going?*
- *What are some things you like about what they provide?*
- *What are some things that you think could be better?*
- *If you could change one thing about their product/service, what would it be?*
- *When was the last time you considered other options in this area?*
- *(Sizing Question) How many _____ do you currently have?*
- *Are you the right person to discuss this area with?*

Just send me your information.
Option 3: Sales Process

> *Sure, I definitely can. Actually, there is a lot of information that I can send over to you. If you have questions about something in particular, it might be easier and quicker to have a brief conversation over the phone on another day instead of me sending over a bunch of information.*

We already use someone for that.
Option 1: Current Environment Questions

> *Oh, great.*

- *Who are you currently using today?*
- *How long have you been with them?*
- *How is everything going?*
- *What are some things you like about what they provide?*
- *What are some things that you think could be better?*
- *If you could change one thing about their product/service, what would it be?*
- *When was the last time you considered other options in this area?*
- *(Sizing Question) How many _____ do you currently have?*
- *Are you the right person to discuss this area with?*

We already use someone for that.
Option 2: Pain Questions

> *Oh, great. If I could ask you real quick:*

- *Pain Question 1*

- *Pain Question 2*
- *Pain Question 3*

We already use someone for that.
Option 3: Pain Points

Oh, great. When I talk with other [Target Buyer Type], they often have challenges with:

- *Pain Point 1*
- *Pain Point 2*
- *Pain Point 3*

Are you concerned about any of those areas?

We do not have budget/money to spend right now.
Option 1: Sales Process

I understand. And I want you to know that I am not reaching out to you to try to sign you up or sell you anything. More so, we are just looking to open the dialogue between our two companies and have an initial conversation.

We would like to learn a little more about you and possibly share some information about us. That way, when you begin your budget planning or when your budget opens back up, you can know who we are and how we can help.

Are you open to having a brief conversation at some point? It does not have to be this week or next, we are not going anywhere.

We do not have budget/money to spend right now.
Option 2: Pain Questions

I understand. If I could ask you real quick:

- *Pain Question 1*
- *Pain Question 2*
- *Pain Question 3*

We do not have budget/money to spend right now.
Option 3: Pain Points

I understand. When I talk with other [Target Buyer Type], they often have challenges with:

- *Pain Point 1*
- *Pain Point 2*
- *Pain Point 3*

Are you concerned about any of those areas?

We are not making any changes right now.
Option 1: Pain Questions

I understand. If I could ask you real quick:

- *Pain Question 1*
- *Pain Question 2*
- *Pain Question 3*

We are not making any changes right now.
Option 2: Current Environment Questions

I understand.

- *Who are you currently using today?*
- *How long have you been with them?*
- *How is everything going?*
- *What are some things you like about what they provide?*
- *What are some things that you think could be better?*
- *If you could change one thing about their product/service, what would it be?*
- *When was the last time you considered other options in this area?*
- *(Sizing Question) How many _____ do you currently have?*
- *Are you the right person to discuss this area with?*

We are not making any changes right now.
Option 3: Pain Points

I understand. When I talk with other [Target Buyer Type], they often have challenges with:

- *Pain Point 1*
- *Pain Point 2*
- *Pain Point 3*

Are you concerned about any of those areas?

We are not making any changes right now.
Option 4: Sales Process

> I understand. And I want you to know that I am not reaching out to you to try to sign you up or sell you anything. More so, we are just looking to open the dialogue between our two companies and have an initial conversation.

> We would like to learn a little more about you and possibly share some information about us. That way, when you ready to make a change, you can know who we are and how we can help.

> Are you open to having a brief conversation at some point? It does not have to be this week or next, we are not going anywhere.

Call me back in X months.
Option 1: Sales Process

> I can certainly do that. But I want you to know that I am not reaching out to you to try to sign you up or sell you anything. More so, we are just looking to open the dialogue between our two companies and have an initial conversation.

> We would like to learn a little more about you and possibly share some information about us. That way, when you ready to look closer at this, you can know who we are and how we can help.

> Are you open to having a brief conversation at some point? It does not have to be this week or next, we are not going anywhere.

Call me back in X months.
Option 2: Customer Specific Pain Points

I can certainly do that. But when we last spoke, you mentioned you had challenges with:

- *Customer concern 1*
- *Customer concern 2*
- *Customer concern 3*

Are you sure it makes sense to put off talking for another X months with those going on?

CHAPTER 15

Meeting Scripts

We can use your sales message and building blocks to create meeting scripts that you can use as a guide and structure for your meetings with prospects.

First Appointment Script

This is a script that you can use when meeting with a prospect in an appointment. We will talk more about how to structure your appointments in Chapter 16 when we discuss managing the different steps of your sales process.

Meeting Warm-Up Questions

- *How is your day going so far?*
- *[Ask a question regarding the weather, sports, recent current event, etc.]*
- *How long have you been working here?*
- *What did you do before this?*
- *Where are you from?*
- *What do you like most about what you do?*
- *I know why I wanted to meet with you. Is there anything that motivated you to want to meet with me?*
- *[Share agenda for meeting] Does that match up with your expectations for this meeting?*

- *Is there anything in particular that you are hoping to get out of this meeting?*
- *Do you have a hard stop for this meeting?*

Current Environment Questions

- *Who are you currently using today?*
- *How long have you been with them?*
- *How is everything going?*
- *What are some things you like about what they provide?*
- *What are some things that you think could be better?*
- *If you could change one thing about their product/service, what would it be?*
- *When was the last time you considered other options in this area?*
- *(Sizing Question) How many _____ do you currently have?*
- *Are you the right person to discuss this area with?*

Pain Questions

If I could ask you real quick:

- *Pain Question 1*
- *Pain Question 2*
- *Pain Question 3*

Pain Points

When I talk with other [Target Buyer Type], they often have challenges with:

- *Pain Point 1*
- *Pain Point 2*
- *Pain Point 3*

Are you concerned about any of those areas?

Product

We provide [Product Name] and that includes:

- *Feature 1*
- *Feature 2*
- *Feature 3*

Benefits

Our [Product Name] can help [Target Buyer Type] to:

- *Value Point 1*
- *Value Point 2*
- *Value Point 3*

Differentiation

Some ways that we differ from other options out there are:

- *Differentiation 1*
- *Differentiation 2*
- *Differentiation 3*

Impact of Doing Nothing

Some things to be concerned about when not doing anything in this area are:

- *Pain Point 1*
- *Pain Point 2*
- *Pain Point 3*

Company Bragging Points

Other key details about us are:

- *Company Fact 1*
- *Company Fact 2*
- *Company Fact 3*

Name Drop

- *We worked with [Customer Name] and helped them to [Technical Improvement].*
- *We were able to do this by providing our [Product Name].*
- *This ultimately helped them to [Business Improvement].*

Qualifying Questions

Need vs. Want

- *What motivated you to look at us (brought you to us)?*
- *Do you mind if I ask why you took time out of your schedule to meet with us?*
- *What improvements could you see if you make this purchase?*
- *What will happen if you do not purchase something?*
- *Is there a date when this purchase needs to be made?*
- *What happens if the purchase is not made by that date?*
- *What is the time frame that the project needs to work along?*

Funding Availability

- What is the budgetary range that you need this purchase to stay within?
- Is there a budget approved for this project?
- Have the funds been allocated to this purchase?
- What budget (department) will this purchase be made under?
- Are there other purchases that this funding may end up being used for?
- How does the project fit with other initiatives from a priority standpoint?

Decision Authority

- What is the decision-making process?
- What parties will be involved in making the decision?
- What are the key factors that a decision will be based on?
- What functional areas (departments) will be impacted by the purchase?
- Is there a committee that this type of purchase has to go through?
- Who is the ultimate decision maker?
- Who is the person that will need to sign the agreement/contract?

Level of Competition

- What other options are you considering?
- How far along are you in discussions with them?
- How do you feel about your other options?
- What do you like about them?
- What do you not like about them?
- How do they compare with what we have to offer?
- Is there a reason why you would choose us over them?
- If you had to make a decision today, which way would you lean?

Closing Questions

Trial Closing

- What do you think about what you have seen so far?
- How do you think this fits with what you are needing?
- How would that feature help you?

- *Is this something you could see your organization using?*
- *Are we heading in the right direction?*
- *Is this what you were expecting to see?*

Soft Closing
- *What would you like to do next?*
- *What direction do you want to go from here?*
- *Do you want to continue talking about this?*
- *When would you like to talk again?*
- *What does the path forward look like?*

Hard Closing
- *Are you ready to move forward to the next step in the process?*
- *What would you need to be able to make a commitment to move forward?*
- *If you had everything that you are asking for, are you prepared to move forward?*
- *When are you going to make your final decision?*
- *(If delaying the decision for a period of time) OK, but do you mind if I ask if there will be a change or something different at that time that will make that a better time to look at moving forward?*
- *Is there anything that is preventing you from being able to move forward with this purchase?*

Networking Meeting Script

This is a script that you can use when meeting with someone you met at a networking event. We will talk more about networking in Chapter 25.

Networking Questions

- *How is your day going so far?*
- *What do you do?*
- *How long have you been doing that?*

- *What did you do before?*
- *What do you like most about what you do?*
- *Is there something that motivated you to get into that type of work?*
- *Where are you from?*
- *What brought you to this event?*
- *Have you found this to be a productive event for you?*
- *Are there any other networking events that you recommend?*
- *How can I help you to be successful?*
- *What does a good prospect look like for you?*

Current Environment Questions

- *Who are you currently using today?*
- *How long have you been with them?*
- *How is everything going?*
- *What are some things you like about what they provide?*
- *What are some things that you think could be better?*
- *If you could change one thing about their product/service, what would it be?*
- *When was the last time you considered other options in this area?*
- *(Sizing Question) How many _____ do you currently have?*
- *Are you the right person to discuss this area with?*

Pain Questions

If I could ask you real quick:

- *Pain Question 1*
- *Pain Question 2*
- *Pain Question 3*

Pain Points

When I talk with other [Target Buyer Type], they often have challenges with:

- *Pain Point 1*
- *Pain Point 2*
- *Pain Point 3*

Are you concerned about any of those areas?

Product

We provide [Product Name] and that includes:

- *Feature 1*
- *Feature 2*
- *Feature 3*

Benefits

Our [Product Name] can help [Target Buyer Type] to:

- *Value Point 1*
- *Value Point 2*
- *Value Point 3*

Differentiation

Some ways that we differ from other options out there are:

- *Differentiation 1*
- *Differentiation 2*
- *Differentiation 3*

Impact of Doing Nothing
Some things to be concerned about when not doing anything in this area are:

- *Pain Point 1*
- *Pain Point 2*
- *Pain Point 3*

Company Bragging Points
Other key details about us are:

- *Company Fact 1*
- *Company Fact 2*
- *Company Fact 3*

Name Drop

- *We worked with [Customer Name] and helped them to [Technical Improvement].*
- *We were able to do this by providing our [Product Name].*
- *This ultimately helped them to [Business Improvement].*

Close

- What is the best way to work together?
- What is the best way to stay in touch?
- When would you like to meet again?

Sales Presentation Outline

This is a rough outline of how you can use your building blocks to create a sales presentation that you can deliver to prospects. You will probably want to add more information to this outline and should use this as more of a starting place that you can build on top of.

Common Challenges

- Pain Point 1
- Pain Point 2
- Pain Point 3

How We Help

- Value Point 1
- Value Point 2
- Value Point 3

Our Products and Services

- Product 1
- Product 2
- Product 3

What We Do

- Feature 1
- Feature 2
- Feature 3

How We Differ

- Differentiation 1
- Differentiation 2
- Differentiation 3

Company Facts

- Company Fact 1
- Company Fact 2
- Company Fact 3

How We Have Helped Others Like You

- We worked with [Customer Name] and helped them to [Technical Improvement].
- We were able to do this by providing our [Product Name].
- This ultimately helped them to [Business Improvement].

Partnership Plan

Activity	Due Date	Owner	Status
Initial Meeting	11/05/2019	Michael Jones Dennis Martin	Complete
Presentation / Demonstration	11/16/2019	Michael Jones Dennis Martin Veronica Flores	Complete
Discovery Meeting	11/23/2019	Michael Jones Stan Wilson	Open
X Corp to provide requirements	11/29/2019	Stan Wilson	Open
Presentation of draft proposal and contract language	12/2/2019	Michael Jones	Open
Communication of change requests to documents	12/5/2019	Dennis Martin	Open
Delivery of final executable documents	12/12/2019	Michael Jones	Open
Partnership agreement signed	12/19/2019	Tech Bee / X Corp	Open
Implementation begins	1/15/2020	Tech Bee / X Corp	Open
Go live	4/1/2020	X Corp	Open

LEVEL 3—SALES TACTICS AND PROCESSES

CHAPTER 16

Managing the Sales Process

In this chapter, we will try to improve how you view and manage the sales process that you take prospects through. Many salespeople might not see this as an area that needs attention because they believe that once they are engaged with a prospect, they can easily figure out what to do next and what direction to take conversations, and that they don't need any type of plan or structure in terms of a process. In other words, it is all about getting the conversation started and then just pushing the prospects as far as they can go in each discussion.

The problem with that way of thinking is that the sales process and steps that you are trying to take a prospect through should play a significant role in what you say because it can impact the questions you ask, the way you respond to objections, and what you try to close the prospect for. With that, this is one of the most important chapters in this book, and just about everything that we discuss after this will point back to the concepts explained in this chapter.

Sales Process Steps

Each product can have a unique sales process, so it is difficult for us to tell you all the individual steps you should take a prospect through from beginning to end. But there are three main steps that a salesperson should go through for most products and these are Initial Contact, Meeting, and Presentation.

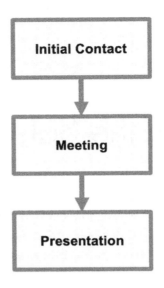

INITIAL CONTACT

The first sales process step is the Initial Contact. This is basically the first time that you interact with the prospect, and this can take place in any of the following formats:

- **Cold call:** You are talking to the prospect on a cold call.

- **Inbound call:** The prospect calls you or your company by either finding you on the internet or being referred to you.

- **Cold email:** You send a cold email to a prospect, and the prospect replies.

- **Inbound email:** The prospect contacts you through your website or sends you an email, and you reply to the email.

- **Website chat:** The prospect contacts your company through a website chat tool.

- **Social media:** You communicate with a prospect through a social media platform.

- **Networking:** You meet and talk with the prospect during a networking event.

I give you this list of types of events so you can see that the Initial Contact step of the sales process is simply the first time that you interact with a prospect, and it can occur in a lot of different ways.

Amount of Time for the Initial Contact

One of the main details to keep in mind with the Initial Contact sales process step is that it should only be between two to five minutes in duration. However, you can easily find yourself talking to a prospect in the first interaction for longer than five minutes. This means you are either spending more time than you should in the Initial Contact or that you have progressed to the next step in the sales process, which is the Meeting. It is OK to talk longer and flow from the Initial Contact to the Meeting in the same interaction, but you should know where you are in the sales process so that you can stay aware of what you need to accomplish as each sales process step has its own goals and objectives.

Goals for the Initial Contact

Here are some of the main things you should try to accomplish during the Initial Contact sales step:

- **Pre-qualify the prospect:** Try to determine if the prospect has at least a slight need or fit with what you sell.

- **Build interest in your product:** Try to create a little interest and curiosity in the product you sell and the company that you work for. However, you do not need to build interest to a level where the prospect wants to purchase your product; you only need to get the prospect interested enough so that her or she is open to talking more.

- **Close the prospect on the next step of the sales process:** Close the prospect on agreeing to move to the Meeting sales process step (set the appointment, schedule the meeting, etc.).

Distribution of Attention

A product selling salesperson primarily talks about his or her own "stuff." To be more of a consultative salesperson, focus more on the prospect and less on you. With that, try to make 80 percent of the Initial Contact step about the prospect and 20 percent about you, your company, and your product.

The way to apply this is to focus the majority of the interaction on the prospect by asking questions to learn more about what is going on with him or her. You can then wrap up the interaction by sharing just enough information about your product and company so that you are able to close the prospect on talking more by moving to the next step in your sales process.

Questions to Ask

You only have a few minutes to work with in the Initial Contact step, so you probably have enough time to ask between two to four questions. Since this is the first time you are speaking with the prospect, you don't want to ask anything too deep or detailed, so a couple of your pain and current environment questions should work best. If you ask a question that uncovers a pain or concern, you can then wrap up your questions and move on to try to close the prospect for talking more and moving forward to the Meeting sales process step.

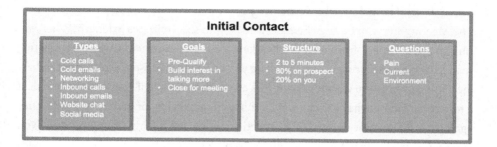

MEETING

The second step in the sales process is the Meeting. This is simply progressing from the very short exchange during the Initial Contact to having a longer and more established conversation. The Meeting step can be in the form of any of the following:

- **Appointment:** You schedule an appointment with a prospect, and that could either be in person, on the phone, or in an online setting.

- **Meet for coffee, drink, or meal:** You meet with the prospect at a neutral location.

- **Extended cold call:** You can transition to the Meeting during a cold call and meet over the phone.

- **Meet at event:** If you meet a prospect at an event, you can progress to the Meeting sales step at that same event.

I give you this list to demonstrate that once you transition to a longer and more established conversation, you are progressing to the Meeting step of the sales process. The more you are aware of this transition, the more able you will be to focus on the goals and objectives for that particular step in the sales process.

Length of Time for the Meeting

The Meeting step can be anywhere between ten to sixty minutes in length. When setting an appointment from a cold call, asking for a fifteen-to-twenty-minute meeting seems to be a good amount of time where you can get the prospect to commit to having a real conversation without asking for too much time. And if you send the prospect a formal calendar invite, you can send a thirty-minute calendar invite even when they agree to a fifteen-to-twenty-minute meeting. If you sell a fairly simple product, you could probably ask for a five-to-ten-minute meeting or call. If you have a fairly complex product and you know that you will have a number of different questions, you may want to position the meeting as a thirty-to-sixty-minute discussion and put the full sixty minutes on the prospect's calendar. However, you will have to build a little more interest and rapport with the prospect in order to get him or her to agree to a sixty-minute block of time for a first meeting.

Goals for the Meeting

It can be easy for a salesperson to think that if a prospect agrees to meet, that prospect must be interested in buying the product, so the salesperson can just show up for the meeting and sell the product. But it is still too early for that type of expectation, and these are the things that you should focus on during the Meeting sales process step:

- **Gather information:** The Meeting is one of your best opportunities to learn about the prospect, and one of your main goals should be to gather information.

- **Qualify the prospect:** This is where you need to start to qualify the prospect to determine if he or she really fits with what you sell and if the prospect will have a decent chance of purchasing from you.

- **Build interest in your product:** Try to create more interest in the product you sell and the company that you work for. However, you do not need to build interest to a level where the prospect wants to purchase your product; you only need to get the prospect interested enough so that he or she is open to learning more about what you have to offer.

- **Close the prospect on the next step:** The close is to get the prospect to agree to move to the Presentation sales process step.

Distribution of Attention

When you reach the Meeting sales step, the balance of attention can level out with you focusing 50 percent of the attention on the prospect and the other 50 percent on you. A good way to do that is to make the first half of the Meeting about the prospect and the second half about you.

Questions to Ask

Here are some of the different types of questions that you could ask in the Meeting:

- **Current Environment Questions:** These are good questions to ask early in the Meeting as they can be a great way to show curiosity and learn what is currently going on with the prospect.

- **Pain Questions:** The Meeting is the best place to ask as many of your pain questions that you can.

- **Qualifying Questions:** The Meeting is the best place for you to determine if the prospect has a good chance of buying from you and your qualifying questions will help you to do that.

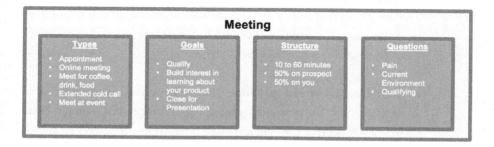

PRESENTATION

The third step in the sales process is the Presentation, and this is where you will go into more detail on what you have to offer the prospect. For many situations, this may be an actual presentation of slides and possibly a demonstration of the product. But there are also many products where there is not much to show or demonstrate, and this step could simply be presenting a proposal, quotation, or list of options.

Length of Time for the Presentation

The Presentation could be as long as one to two hours for products that require a formal presentation or demonstration. If it is more of a presentation of pricing or options, it could be a ten-to-thirty-minute conversation.

Goals for the Presentation

The Presentation is basically your opportunity to tell the prospect what you have to offer and why they should buy from you. Here are some of the key things you should try to accomplish:

- **Show how you can help:** Hopefully by this point you have figured out what the prospect wants, needs, or is having challenges with. Spend this time explaining how you match up with that.

- **Continue to qualify the prospect:** Going into the Presentation sales step, you should have a pretty good idea of how qualified the prospect is. But you can use some of this time to learn more about the prospect in order to qualify him or her even further.

- **Build interest in your product:** The Presentation is your main opportunity to build the prospect's interest in purchasing your product. This is where you need to communicate what you have to offer, how it can help the prospect, and why the prospect should purchase from you.

- **Close the prospect on the sale:** This is where you should try to close the prospect on moving forward with the purchase of your product. Even if there are more sales process steps after the Presentation, this is where you want to get some sort of close or validation in terms of the prospect's interest and intent to move forward.

Distribution of Attention

In the Presentation, we will flip the distribution of attention from what it was in the Initial Contact of 80 percent on the prospect and 20 percent on you and change it to 20 percent on the prospect and 80 percent on you. What that might look like is that if you schedule a sixty-minute meeting with the prospect, you can spend the first five to ten minutes summarizing what you learned about the prospect, you can then spend forty to fifty minutes talking about what you have to offer and how you can help, and then end the meeting with five to ten minutes back on the prospect as you try to close and identify the path forward.

Questions to Ask

If you are going through these sales steps in order, you may have already asked a lot of questions prior to this step, so there could be a situation where you do not have any questions to ask. But you should try to take advantage of every meeting and conversation that you have with the prospect to learn more. With that, you can certainly ask any of your pain questions, current environment questions, or qualifying questions at any point during the Presentation.

Toward the end of the Presentation step is where you should most likely begin to try to close the prospect on his or her level of interest and intent to purchase your product. As part of that, you should ask some of your qualifying and closing questions.

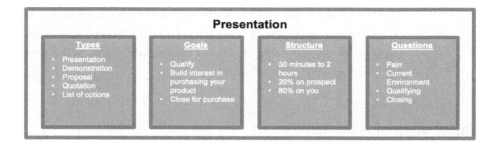

How These Steps Can Be Put Together

We just outlined three sales process steps that you can try to take a prospect through. And while we explain them in a way where the steps are three completely separate interactions that you can have with the prospect, there are certainly a few different ways that you can take a prospect through them.

Each Step on a Different Day

The default or standard way to use these steps is that each step happens on a separate day. This is where you have the Initial Contact with the prospect on one day, have the Meeting on another day, and then have the Presentation on another day. This is a fairly good way to go and will work for most products.

Instant Meeting

There is a scenario where you have the Initial Contact with a prospect and the Meeting ends up happening at the same time. For example, you cold call a prospect and then end up talking to them for twenty minutes. We refer to this as an Instant Meeting.

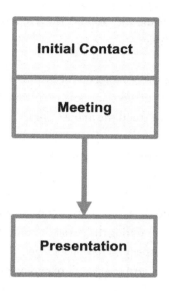

Here are some factors to consider that make it ideal to try to have Instant Meetings:

- Your prospect is extremely difficult to get a hold of, and you do not know if you will ever get him or her on the phone again.

- Your Initial Contact is a face-to-face conversation, and it is easier to just have the Meeting at the same time.

- Your product is fairly simple and there is no need to meet again on a different day.

- Your prospect wants to move quickly.

The Accidental Instant Meeting

While those are good reasons to have an Instant Meeting, there can be cases where you accidentally flow into an Instant Meeting by talking to a prospect in the Initial Contact, and the next thing you know, you have talked for twenty to thirty minutes.

Be careful to not accidentally let your Initial Contact interaction flow into an Instant Meeting because there are some very good reasons to try to draw a line between the Initial Contact and the Meeting:

- When you put the Meeting on the prospect's calendar for a different day, you usually end up getting more time and attention from the prospect than if you just extend the Initial Contact.

- When you have the Meeting on another day, this will give both you and the prospect time to become more prepared for the longer conversation.

- Sometimes you flow into an Instant Meeting because the prospect asks a lot of questions during the Initial Contact. This is a missed opportunity to close the prospect on having a longer discussion on a different day so that you can get into the details regarding his or her questions.

If you start to feel like the Initial Contact is flowing into an Instant Meeting, you should check in with the prospect and close for the Meeting step, and here are a couple of ways to do that:

Close for Meeting When Prospect Asks Questions

That is a great question, and it is probably a bit of a discussion to explain. Do you want to have a larger conversation to discuss that question and any others you may have? We can schedule another call since I called you out of the blue. Or we can keep talking right now if you have another twenty minutes to get into some of the details.

Close for Meeting When Getting into Details

We are starting to get into some of the technical details here, and I just want to check in with you since I called you out of the blue. Do you want to discuss this in more detail now, or would it make sense

*for us to schedule a call or meeting on another day where I can put
some time on your calendar and we can get into all of the details?*

INSTANT PRESENTATION

There is another scenario where you have the Initial Contact and the Meeting on two separate days, but the Meeting flows into the Presentation. What this might look like is that you have a meeting with a prospect and end up showing the information from the Presentation step toward the end of the Meeting.

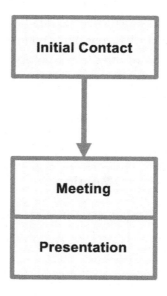

Similar to the Instant Meeting, the same factors apply that would make this a good thing to do. But if those are not at play, it is probably best to have your Presentation on a different day.

One Call Close

There are some salespeople who would see the three sales process steps and say that they do not fit with what they sell because their product is very simple and can be sold through a one call close process. While I do agree that some products are simple and don't need all of these different steps on different days, it still makes sense to go through the three sales process steps, even if all of the steps occur in the same interaction. In other words, it might look like one call and one step, but you are still taking the prospect through the three different sales process steps.

For example, if you cold call a prospect, the first two to five minutes of the call is the Initial Contact. During this step, you ask a couple of questions and then get the prospect to agree to talk a little more. After that point, you have just transitioned to the Meeting step. For the next five to ten minutes, you learn a little about the prospect and share a few more details about your product. You then get the prospect to agree to hear your different options, and you have just transitioned to the Presentation. At this point, you share three packages that the prospect can choose from, and you close the prospect on agreeing to purchase one of the options. You have just performed a one call close and went through all three sales process steps.

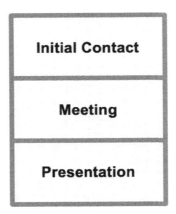

While that example may also be viewed as a single sales process step, by being aware that it is three different steps, you will have more control of the conversation and more clarity for what you need to say, ask, and do.

CHAPTER 17

Cold Calling

Cold calling can be one of the most difficult tasks that a salesperson has to perform because you never really know what direction a cold call will go, you only have a small window of time to work with, and there is a very good chance you are going to face some sort of resistance on every call. In this chapter, we will explain a process for making cold calls that minimizes those challenges, and this will not only make cold calling easier, but it should also improve your results as well.

Cold Call Process

The SMART Sales System process for cold calling is flexible and provides clarity for what to do in all of the different directions that a call can go. We are able to do this by breaking the cold call down into different blocks to create an outline of different things you can talk about with a prospect:

- Open the Call
- Purpose of the Call
- Sales Takeaway
- Pre-Qualify
- Pain Points
- Product
- Close

It would never make sense to try to go through each of these blocks and share each point with the prospect because you do not have enough time for that. More so, this is a modular design and you should start at the top and can bounce around according to how the call goes. This allows the cold call script to be flexible and provides options for most of the different directions that a call can go.

Here is a step-by-step process for how to go through these blocks and this process provides logic for where to go next depending on how the prospect responds.

STEP 1: OPENING THE CALL

One way that salespeople often start out a cold call is by saying something like this:

> *Hello, [Contact's Name]. This is [Salesperson's Name] with [Salesperson's Company]. How are you doing today?*

I believe that the question of "how are you doing today" is not a great way to start a call because it can make you look like a salesperson who is trying to sell something, and only asking how the prospect is doing to try to manufacture rapport. With that, make one small change and replace the question of "how are you doing today" with a question to confirm availability with something like this:

> *Hello, [Contact's Name]. This is [Your Name] with [Your Company]. Have I caught you in the middle of anything?*

This one small change can make a huge difference in how the call goes for the following reasons:

- **Improve the first impression you make:** You will look less like a salesperson and more like someone who is more familiar, casual, consultative, and confident.

- **Decrease resistance from the prospect:** Because you look less like a salesperson, your prospect will be less defensive, and this may decrease the objections that you have to face.

- **Confirm availability:** This will help you to determine if the prospect is available for your call.

- **Buy yourself window of time:** When you are able to confirm that the prospect is not in the middle of anything, you have just bought yourself a few minutes of time to work with for your cold call.

- **Build rapport:** Opening a call in this way is casual, friendly, polite, and respectful. This will help you to start building rapport at the very beginning of your first time speaking with the prospect.

Where to Go Next in the Process

There are two directions you can go after this step in this process:

- **Advance to Step 2:** If the prospect answers with anything close to the following, move forward to Step 2.

Yes, but I am OK.
No, I am fine.
It depends. Why are you calling?
What is this call in regards to?

- **Deflect to an objection response:** If the prospect responds with anything close to the following, you can respond with the following objection response.

Yes, I am in the middle of something.
I am busy right now.
I am not available.

151

Salesperson Response:

Oh, OK. I can be very brief, or I can call you back at another time. Which do you prefer?

or

Oh, OK. When is the best time for me to call you back?

STEP 2: STATE THE PURPOSE OF YOUR CALL

The next step is to state the purpose of your call. And since technically you are a salesperson who is trying to sell something, the purpose of your call could be to:

- Introduce yourself and your company
- Schedule an appointment or meeting
- Learn about the prospect's needs
- Share details about the product that you have to offer
- Sell your product to the prospect

But since you don't want to sound like a salesperson who is trying to sell something, do not share any of those as the purpose of your call as it will trigger guardedness and objections. With that, simply share either your value points, pain points, or name-drop building blocks as the reason for your call, and this can look something like this:

Value Points

Great. The reason for my call is that we help [Target Buyer Type] to:

- *Value Point 1*
- *Value Point 2*
- *Value Point 3*

Pain Points

Great. The reason for my call is that we help [Target Buyer Type] with the challenges of:

- *Pain Point 1*
- *Pain Point 2*
- *Pain Point 3*

Name-Drop

Great. The reason for my call is that:

- *We worked with [Customer Name] and helped them to [Technical Improvement].*
- *This ultimately helped them to [Business Improvement].*

Where to Go Next in the Process

After you share your purpose of the call, advance to Step 3.

STEP 3: DELIVER A SOFT SALES TAKEAWAY (OPTIONAL)

This next step is to perform a soft sales takeaway, and that can be sharing one of the following:

Sales Takeaway

- *I do not know if you need what we provide.*
- *I do not know if you are a good fit with what we do.*

- *I do not know if we can help you in the same way that we have helped others.*
- *I do not know if you are interested in those improvements.*
- *I do not know if you are concerned about those areas.*
- *I do not know if you are the right person to speak with.*
- *I do not know if it makes sense for us to talk.*

Most of the salespeople that your prospects talk to will always be trying to sell and get the prospect to move forward. The sales takeaway is the complete opposite of that, and it will help to disarm prospects' guardedness. This tells prospects that you are not going to push something on them and that you are looking out for their best interest. Not only can this help you to minimize objections and establish the call, it can also help to build rapport and trust.

This step is completely optional, and if you don't like this or it does not fit with your selling style, simply skip this step and advance to Step 4.

Where to Go Next in the Process
After you deliver a soft sales takeaway, advance to Step 4.

STEP 4: PRE-QUALIFY

The next step is to ask a few questions to try to pre-qualify the prospect to determine if there is even the slightest fit between what he or she needs and what you have to of-fer. For example, if you were a doctor talking to a patient on the phone, to pre-qualify might be to first see how the patient feels because if he or she feels good or great, it does not make sense to talk. But if the doctor can identify that the patient feels bad or just OK, then there is a reason to talk a little more because the doctor can possibly help the patient to feel better.

The best way to pre-qualify the prospect is to simply ask a few of your pain and current environment questions as these are very effective and efficient at identifying how the prospect is doing in the areas that your product helps.

How to View the Prospect's Answers

In order to pre-qualify the prospect, listen to his or her answers and determine if what is said makes the person a good or bad prospect for you. If he or she responds in a way where it sounds like things are just OK or could be better, you have just identified that it might make sense to talk more, and you can use that to justify closing the prospect on moving to the next step in your sales process.

If you want to make this a little more systematic, here are three categories that you could put the prospect's response into:

1. **Hot response:** This is like hitting a jackpot in a casino with the lights going off because the prospect answers that he or she is not doing great in the area where you have something to offer. This would be like a doctor identifying that the patient has the key symptoms for the medicine he or she has to offer.

2. **Neutral response:** This is where the prospect does not know how he or she is doing in the area that you help with or that things are just OK. This would be where a patient does not have symptoms or feel sick, but also cannot say that he or she feels great either.

3. **Cold response:** This is where the prospect responds in a way where it appears that things are pretty good or even great. This would be where a doctor asks how a patient is doing, and the patient has no symptoms and is in the best shape of his or her life.

If you are able to put the prospect's answer into one of those categories, you can then follow these rules for what to do next on the call:

1. **Hot response:** If you get a hot response, you can skip ahead in the script and try to close for the next step of the sales process (the Meeting) because there is a match with what he or she needs and how you help.

2. **Neutral response:** If you get a neutral response, you can move forward to ask another question to see if you can get a better answer. If you have asked a couple of questions and they are all neutral, you can move forward to the very next step in the process, which is sharing common pain points to see if you can get a better response from the prospect. You can also treat neutral responses as you would hot responses, since the prospect is not able to say that things are good or great. With that logic, you could try to close for the next step in the sales process because it could make sense to talk more.

3. **Cold response:** If you get a cold response, you can move forward to ask another question to see if you can get a better answer. If you have asked a couple of questions and they are all cold, you can advance to the next step in the cold call process.

Benefits to Asking Questions

Asking good questions at this point in the call can improve your cold calls in the following ways:

- Helps to make the call more about the prospect and his or her interests than about you and your product
- Gets the prospect more engaged in the conversation
- Helps you to extract valuable information—knowledge is power
- Makes you seem more professional and consultative—more as a consultant or businessperson than a salesperson
- Makes you seem more trustworthy because you are asking questions before trying to sell something
- Helps to build rapport as it shows you care more about the prospect and want to learn about him or her

One thing to keep in mind is that you only have two to five minutes to work with, so you only have enough time to ask a few questions. Anything more than that and you are taking too much time for the Initial Contact. If you ask more questions and actually get the prospect talking a lot, you might have progressed into an Instant Meeting.

Where to Go Next in the Process

Here are two different directions you can go with the cold call based on what happens in this step:

- **Advance to Step 6:** If you get an answer that is an indicator that the prospect might have pain or be a fit for what you sell, you could try to use that answer to skip ahead in this cold call process and try to go for the close. To do this, after you hear a hot or neutral response to one of your questions, you can say something like this:

  Well, based on what you shared, it might make sense for us to talk in more detail because that is the type of thing that we help with.

  After you say that, you can skip ahead and advance to Step 6 where you can share some details from your product building block. The logic here is that right before you try to close the prospect, you need to share some of the details about your product and company so that you can build enough interest to get the prospect to agree to move to the next step in your sales process (the Meeting).

- **Advance to Step 5:** If you don't get much to work with from the prospect's answers, you could advance to Step 5.

STEP 5: SHARE PAIN POINTS

If your questions are not able to identify that the prospect has any pain or concerns, you can try to take a more direct approach and just ask if he or she has any of the problems that you help to resolve with something like this:

Pain Points

When I talk with other [Target Buyer Type], they often have challenges with:

- *Pain Point 1*
- *Pain Point 2*
- *Pain Point 3*

Are you concerned about any of those areas?

The way to use the pain points block in your cold call is that it is basically your fallback position when nothing else is working. The initial strategy is to uncover problems, challenges, or concerns with your questions to create a reason to talk more. But it is very reasonable to not find areas that need improvement because either the questions are not perfect, the prospect is not aware of pain, the prospect is not being honest, or there is no pain. If your questions don't uncover anything, you can use this as one last attempt before starting to move on.

An example of this could be a doctor who asks a patient a few questions to probe for different symptoms. If every question gets an answer that the patient is good, the doctor could share a list of symptoms with the patient and very directly ask if he or she has any of the symptoms before giving the patient a clean bill of health.

Where to Go Next in the Process

Here are two different directions you can go with the cold call based on what happens in this step:

- **Advance to Step 6:** If you identify that the prospect has a problem or concern, you have a reason to talk more, and you can respond with something like:

  Well, based on what you shared, it might make sense for us to talk in more detail because that is the type of thing that we help with.

After you say that, advance to Step 6, which is where you can share some details from your product building block. The logic here is that right before you try to close the prospect, you need to share some details about your product and company so that you can build enough interest to get the prospect to agree to move to the next step in your sales process (the Meeting).

- **Begin to walk away:** If you asked your pain and current environment questions and shared the pain points and the prospect is not expressing any concerns, you might start to walk away by disqualifying the prospect and moving on to find a better prospect. That might look something like this:

Well, it sounds like you all are doing pretty good over there. It might not make much sense for us to talk.

After that, you can either let the prospect go, or, if you want to give it one last attempt, you can still progress to Step 6 to share some info about your product.

STEP 6: SHARE SOME BRIEF PRODUCT AND COMPANY DETAILS

This is where you will share a few brief details about your product and company with the goal of building enough interest so that you are able to close the prospect on moving to the next step in your sales process (the Meeting).

Keep in mind that you are trying to operate in a two-to-five-minute window, so you probably have a minute or less for this step. Which means you can share only a few of these high-level details:

- **Product and features:** Share a couple quick details about your product and what it includes.

159

- **Benefits:** Share some of the improvements that your product can deliver.

- **Differentiation:** Explain how your product is different from the competition.

- **ROI:** Share the type of return the prospect could see from buying your product.

- **Impact of doing nothing:** You can share some of the negative things that can happen if the prospect does not purchase anything.

- **Name-drop example:** Share an example of a customer you helped.

- **Company bragging points:** Share a couple impressive facts about your company.

This is what this might look like:

Product

We provide [Product Name] and that includes:

- *Feature 1*
- *Feature 2*
- *Feature 3*

Benefits
Our [Product Name] can help [Target Buyer Type] to:

- *Value Point 1*
- *Value Point 2*
- *Value Point 3*

Differentiation

Some ways that we differ from other options out there are:

- *Differentiation 1*
- *Differentiation 2*
- *Differentiation 3*

Impact of Doing Nothing

Some things to be concerned about when not doing anything in this area are:

- *Pain Point 1*
- *Pain Point 2*
- *Pain Point 3*

Company Bragging Points

Other key details about us are that we:

- *Company Fact 1*
- *Company Fact 2*
- *Company Fact 3*

Name Drop

- *We worked with [Customer Name] and helped them to [Technical Improvement].*
- *We were able to do this by providing our [Product Name].*
- *This ultimately helped them to [Business Improvement].*

Where to Go Next in the Process

After sharing a few high-level details, move forward to the next step, which is to try to close the prospect.

STEP 7: CLOSE

Hopefully at this point, you have identified that there is a reason to talk more and have also made the prospect a little interested in continuing the conversation. With that, you can try to pause the conversation, check in with the prospect, and confirm if he or she is interested in talking more, and here is what that might look like:

Cold Call Close

But I have called you out of the blue, and I am not sure if this is the best time to discuss this.

Are you interested in discussing this a little more?

Are you available for a brief 15 to 20 minute meeting where I can share some examples of how we have helped other [Target Buyer Type] to:

- *Value Point 1*
- *Value Point 2*
- *Value Point 3*

Or are you available to continue talking about this now?

Where to Go Next in the Process

Here are three different directions you can go with the cold call based on what happens in this step:

- **Confirm the meeting:** If the prospect is interested in talking more, identify if it makes sense to keep talking on the phone or if it is better to get back together on another day. If another day is best, confirm the date, time, and location for that discussion and then send an email and a calendar invite with the meeting information.

- **Go back to your questions:** If the prospect does not agree to talk more, you can keep the call going by bouncing back to Step 4 and asking one of your questions that you did not ask earlier in the call. That could look something like this:

Pain Questions

Oh, I understand. If I could ask you real quick:

- *Pain Question 1*
- *Pain Question 2*
- *Pain Question 3*

Current Environment Questions

Oh, I understand. If I could ask you real quick:

- *Who are you currently using today?*
- *How long have you been with them?*
- *How is everything going?*
- *What are some things you like about what they provide?*
- *What are some things that you think could be better?*
- *If you could change one thing about their product/service, what would it be?*
- *When was the last time you considered other options in this area?*
- *(Sizing Question) How many _____ do you currently have?*
- *Are you the right person to discuss this area with?*

The goal with that tactic would be to find a pain point or concern. If you are successful with that, you can then try to close again with the justification being the new information you uncovered.

- **Go back to your pain points:** Another option is to go back to Step 5 and share some pain points if you skipped over that step earlier in the call. That could look something like this:

Pain Points

Oh, I understand. When I talk with other [Target Buyer Type], they often have challenges with:

- *Pain Point 1*
- *Pain Point 2*
- *Pain Point 3*

Are you concerned about any of those areas?

Does Cold Calling Work?

I often get questions about if cold calling still works or if it still makes sense to do. And sometimes salespeople ask if they can have a successful outbound strategy that only uses email. I like to use a golf analogy to answer those questions.

In golf, you will play a round of golf typically with a bag of different clubs. Each club serves a different purpose by hitting the ball a different distance with a different level of accuracy. For example, a driver hits the ball the farthest but has the worst accuracy. And on the other extreme, the putter hits the ball the shortest distance but is the most accurate. You can view your sales and marketing tools as being similar in that you have many different tools, and each one can deliver your message different distances with different levels of accuracy.

Email marketing and email prospecting might be the equivalent to the driver in that you can send your message to a lot of people very easily and quickly. But in terms of accuracy, it is not great because you don't know who is receiving and reading your emails. And the cold call or the phone is equivalent to the putter. It is the most accurate tool that you have because you end up with direct, person-to-person communication. But the phone is the least efficient because you can only call one person at a time, and it can take a lot of effort and time to get prospects on the phone.

If we go back to golf, you can technically play a round of golf without your putter because you could use other clubs to hit the ball into the hole. But your score will be much worse than it would be if you used the putter because you will not have the accuracy that you need when you are close to the hole. You would also not want to play a round of golf with only your putter as you would lose all of the distance and efficiency that the other clubs provide, and it would take a lot more time and effort to play. This is why it makes sense to have a full set of clubs with some that provide distance and others that provide accuracy.

Similar to playing golf with only a putter, if you try to use a sales strategy that only uses cold calling as your lead generation tool, you will be spending a lot more time and effort for the same (or less) results than you would if you had many different tools. And if you have a strategy that does not include the cold call or phone, your results will be less than what they could be because you will miss a lot of opportunities that could have been closed with the accuracy and deliverability of person-to-person communication. In other words, yes, cold calling works if it is part of a sales strategy that uses many different tools and approaches. If you only do cold calling, because of the effort that you are having to put in, you might feel like it is not working and is a failed approach. And if you don't use some level of cold calling, you will be missing opportunities and not sell as much as you could.

CHAPTER 18

Email Prospecting

In this chapter, we will outline tips and processes to help you with email prospecting.

Using Email Templates

When you are prospecting, you will find yourself in the exact same situations again and again:

- You want to send a cold email to a prospect.
- You just left a prospect a voicemail and need to send a voicemail follow-up email.
- You briefly spoke to a prospect, and he or she asked you to send an email with your information.
- You just had a meeting and need to send a meeting follow-up email.

Since these situations come up again and again, it is a waste of valuable time to write these emails every time you need to send one. With that, you can create email templates for each of these situations, and this will not only save a lot of time, but you can also improve your messages by fine-tuning your email templates over time. These are some of the email templates to create at a bare minimum:

- Cold email templates
- Cold call follow-up email templates
- Voicemail follow-up email templates

- Meeting follow-up email templates

When you send one of these email templates to a prospect, you can certainly edit and customize the message for that particular situation. But to at least have a starting place with a template can help tremendously to improve your efficiency and effectiveness.

Email Prospecting Dos and Dont's

Here are some key dos and don'ts to keep in mind with sending prospecting emails.

DO: UNDERSTAND THE PROSPECT

When creating email messages, always keep in mind two things: 1) the prospect you are emailing is likely extremely busy, and 2) the prospect likely gets a lot of emails from salespeople who are trying to sell something.

DON'T: MOTIVATE THE INSTANTLY DELETE

Since prospects are busy and get sold to a lot, they will likely delete a lot of messages without reading them or reading very little of them, and I call this the "instant delete." While it can be difficult to figure out how to get prospects to respond to your emails, there are some very small and easy changes that can decrease how quickly they delete your emails. In other words, instead of putting all of your attention on how to get prospects to respond to your emails, first start out by trying to prevent prospects from instantly deleting your messages. We outline the small things that will help decrease your instant delete rate in the next few tips.

DO: USE BREVITY WITH YOUR EMAILS

One of the biggest factors that will influence an instant delete is the number of words and length of the email. It is very simple: the longer the email, the more likely the email will be instantly deleted. With that, try to keep your email messages as short as possible in terms of word count and number of sentences to minimize the instant delete rate. After you write an email, look at each word in a similar way to how you might pack a suitcase for a long trip and try to determine if each word is needed in order for you to get your point across. Every word that you are able to delete while keeping your message intact is a step in the right direction for you to decrease the instant delete rate.

DON'T: SOUND LIKE A SALESPERSON

Prospects will be quicker to delete emails from salespeople who appear to be trying to sell something. With that, if you can decrease how much you look like a salesperson in your email, you can decrease how quickly your emails get deleted. In Chapter 3, we discussed product selling and consultative selling. If your emails use more of a product selling sales message, you are more likely to look like a salesperson trying to sell something. By using more of a consultative selling sales message for your emails, you can sound more like a consultant, businessperson, or advisor, and we will show you what that looks like later in this chapter.

DON'T: MAKE IT ALL ABOUT YOU

It can be common for product selling salespeople to send emails that are all about them by focusing on items like this:

- *This is who I am.*
- *This is who I work for.*
- *This is what we do/sell.*
- *Do you need what I sell?*

This type of message is a bit self-absorbed and all about the salesperson's own interests and what he or she cares about. Try to flip that around and instead of being all about you, make your email all about the prospect. The consultative selling sales message will help you to do this by shifting you away from talking about your product and company and focusing more on how you can help the prospect.

DON'T: LOOK LIKE A MASS EMAIL

When you send an email to a list of prospects, try to design your email so that it does not look like a mass email. To give an example of why this can be helpful, think about checking your physical mailbox at your home. When you see an envelope that is professionally printed with different colors and images, you know that you can throw it away without looking at it because it is an advertisement or piece of direct mail trying to sell something.

Now picture getting an envelope that is very plain and has your address written by hand. You may be much slower to throw this piece of mail away because it appears to be one-to-one, and you might miss something important if you throw it away because this message was sent only to you. By making your email look more one-to-one and less one-to-many, you can decrease the instant delete rate.

The main way to do this is to minimize how much you try to make the email look nice with extra formatting and design improvements. The logic is that when someone sends a one-to-one email, he or she will spend less time working on the cosmetics of an email than a salesperson who is creating an email that will be sent out to a list of prospects. Here are some examples of the small formatting changes that someone might do to make an email look better:

- Using a hyperlink (click here to sign up) instead of writing out a website (www.salesscripter.com/signup)
- Formatting text with bold and italicized styles
- Inserting images, graphics, borders, shading, etc.

When an email has a lot of extra formatting, it can give the impression that someone created an email template and is blasting it out to many different people. This impression can make someone feel that it is OK to instantly delete an email message.

DON'T: SELL THE PRODUCT, SELL THE MEETING

A lot of salespeople focus their email messages on the ultimate goal of selling the product. For example, if a salesperson that sells web design services sends an email asking if the prospect needs a new website, this message is focused on the ultimate goal of selling the prospect a new website. Even though the salesperson cannot close the sale through the email message, the salesperson has still written their message around the ultimate goal of selling the product.

This salesperson could greatly improve his or her email prospecting by simply shifting from selling the product (website design) and focus more on selling the meeting. The web design salesperson could focus on selling a conversation to talk about websites and offer to share some recommendations and examples of how the prospect could improve their current website. Not only does this decrease the instant delete rate, but this is actually a more logical approach because the next thing that is going to happen after an email exchange is a conversation, not a purchase.

In addition, the odds that you send your email at the exact time that the prospect is thinking about buying what you sell is extremely low. This means that, when focusing on the ultimate goal of selling the product, you are trying to hit a very difficult and specific target with the email you are sending. By changing the message and strategy to simply starting the conversation or selling the meeting, you make the target much bigger and this increases the odds of success for your email message and your sales strategy.

DO: USE A MULTITOUCH APPROACH

Because prospects are busy and get a lot of emails from salespeople, it is going to take many different touches in order to get their attention. This means that not only do you have to send multiple emails, but you should also augment your email prospecting with phone calls, voicemails, social media, physical mail, etc.

DO: EDUCATE THE PROSPECT

Since you are going to send multiple emails to the prospect, one thing you can do is break down your sales message into short stories or messages. You can then use each email to tell a different part of your message. With this approach, you can use a series of email messages to educate prospects over a period of time on how you can help them and why they should talk to you.

DON'T: BE APOLOGETIC

Don't apologize in your emails about bothering the prospect. For example, salespeople can often try to soften their email by saying something like:

- *I am sorry to bother you.*
- *I know you are busy.*
- *I won't take too much of your time.*

Not only is this the type of thing that a salesperson who is trying to sell something would say, but this is also very weak and can impact how the prospect views and respects you. You can be respectful of the prospect's time without being apologetic. Be confident in who you are and the value your product delivers. If you had a bag of money to give to someone, would you apologize for bothering them to talk about the bag of money?

DON'T: QUESTION THE PROSPECT ABOUT PREVIOUS EMAILS

Do not ask the prospect if they saw or read the emails you have sent them in the past. For example, some salespeople will send a second email that starts out with something like this:

- *Did you see my last email?*
- *Did you read my last email?*
- *You never replied to my last email.*
- *I never heard back from you on my last email.*

In my opinion, there is little to be gained by knowing whether the prospect has read your last email, and it is actually a little rude to ask about this. This is the type of question that a manager would ask a subordinate when questioning the status of a task or assignment. A salesperson is not the manager of the prospect. If anything, the salesperson is the employee to the prospect or customer. As a result, do not question prospects on whether they have read or seen your emails, and just assume that they have not.

DON'T: ASK THE PROSPECT TO REPLY

Do not ask the prospect to reply to your message with something like this in your message:

I would really appreciate if you would reply to this email.

This is the salesperson asking the prospect to perform a task and the salesperson should not be giving the prospect any type of work to perform at this point in the sales process. Again, the prospect does not work for the salesperson, the salesperson works for the prospect.

Creating Your Email Messages

The first step in creating your prospecting email messages is to brainstorm the different topics to build your email messages around. In order to avoid looking like a salesperson who is trying to sell something, try to minimize how much you talk about your product and company in your prospecting emails. You may wonder what there is left to say if you don't talk about your product and company. The answer to that is that if you are using the consultative selling sales message that we discussed in Chapter 3, you can create email messages using the following building blocks:

- Value Points
- Pain Points
- Pain Questions
- Name-Drop
- Product

One option you have is to create one email for each building block. For example, if your value points are that you help individuals to become healthier, decrease stress, and increase confidence, you could create one email with your value points building block with something like this:

Subject Line: Become healthier and decrease stress

Hello [Contact First Name],

The reason for the email is that we help people to:

- Become healthier
- Decrease stress
- Increase confidence

I don't know if you want to improve those areas and that is why I am reaching out.

Are you available for a brief 15 to 20 minute meeting where I can share some examples of how we have helped people to get healthier?

Best Regards,
[Email Signature]

You may read that email template and think that it is extremely short and does not say much about what the salesperson sells or does. That is correct and on purpose because the email is designed to be very lean on word count and just touch on the value points offered by the product. And because we know that we are going to send more emails to the contact, we do not have to get into all of the details because additional information will be coming later in future emails as we continue to try to contact and educate the prospect.

While the value points email example includes all of the points of a particular building block, you can also create email messages for an individual point as well. For example, if your value points are that you help individuals to become healthier, decrease stress and increase confidence, you could create a message that is built around the value point of decreasing stress, and that could look something like this.

Subject Line: Alternative ways to decrease stress

Hello [Contact First Name],

The reason for the email is that we people to decrease stress and do this through natural and holistic ways.

I don't know if you want to improve that area and that is why I am reaching out.

Are you available for a brief 15 to 20 minute meeting where I can share some examples of how we are helping people to decrease stress?

Best Regards,
[Email Signature]

Creating Email Threads

If you create multiple cold email messages, you can string those together to create an email thread, which is series of emails that are strung together and designed to go out to a prospect over a period of time. Here are some examples of how to structure an email thread using the cold email templates provided in Chapter 12:

- Email 1: Value Points Message
- Email 2: Pain Points Message
- Email 3: Name-Drop Message
- Email 4: Pain Questions Message
- Email 5: Product Message
- Email 6: Last Attempt Message

This email thread example could just be a starting place for you to build on as there are likely additional emails that you can add based on your particular situation. For example, we have a page on our website where visitors can download free ebooks and we added a message to this email thread that mentions our ebooks. We also have a lot of free training videos on YouTube and added a message to this thread that mentions those videos. With those emails added, our email thread is eight email messages. I share this to give you ideas of how you can build on this email thread to make it longer and make it more tailored to what you have to say or offer.

Subject Lines

Instead of trying to figure out what subject line will get the prospect to open and read the email, create a subject line that does not trigger a negative reaction and an instant delete. For that, here are some things I recommend avoiding with your subject lines:

- Words in all caps
- Including exclamation marks
- Using emoticons
- Sharing product details
- Including details about a promotion, discount, or special

Including details like that in your subject line will communicate that you are a salesperson who is trying to sell something, and the prospect will be more motivated to instantly delete your message.

A different way to go is to use a subject line that is more subtle and simply says something about the general direction or angle you are coming from. Using one of your value points or pain points as a subject line can sometimes be a good way to share what you are emailing about without sounding too much like a salesperson who is trying sell something. For example, if one of your value points is that you help to decrease the amount of time it takes to train new sales hires, you could turn that into "Decrease training time for new sales hires" as your subject line. Of if you help with the pain point that it can take a long time to onboard new sales hires, you could turn that into "Time consuming to get new sales hires ramped up."

While neither of those are real creative or flashy, they communicate the general area that you are wanting to talk about without setting off the alarm that you are a salesperson who is trying to sell something.

Sending Your Emails

Once you have created your email messages, you could certainly just send them out of your business email inbox one at a time. But there are a lot of tools and techniques to make that more efficient and here are some things you may want to consider.

AUTOMATE THE DELIVERY OF YOUR EMAILS

Time is your most valuable asset as a salesperson. You can buy more materials and hire more people, but you cannot buy more time or add more hours to the week. With that, I suggest that you automate as much of your sales activities that you can, and one of the easiest things to automate is the delivery of your emails. And you can automate your emails in two ways:

- **Email scheduling:** There are many email automation tools that allow you to automate a series of emails to go out over a period of time in a "set it and forget it" type of design.

- **Mass email blasts:** Many of the same systems that will help you to automate the delivery of your emails will also allow you to send out an email to a list of contacts all at the same time in a mass blast type of process.

I highly recommend that you implement tools like this because it is similar to cloning yourself where the software is doing part of your job for you. This will help you to scale your sales efforts and allow you to spend time on other tasks while the software is doing part of your job for you.

TRACK THE EMAILS YOU SEND

If possible, try to use some sort of tool to track the emails you send in order to collect data on which prospects opened your emails and clicked on the links. This data can be extremely valuable as it can tell you which prospects are engaging with your emails and who you should spend your valuable time calling. Just about all of the email automation systems will provide this type of tracking functionality.

LEAD SCORING

If you are using a system for tracking email opens and links clicked, try to find a system that will associate points with those actions so that you can do lead scoring. For example, in the SalesScripter software application, prospects that you email will get quality points for email opens and links clicked (one point for an email open and three points for a link clicked). With this type of functionality, as you continue to send your different email messages to prospects, the points will start accruing for prospects who are engaging with your emails. You can then use this data to clearly see which prospects it makes sense for you to cold call.

TIMING FOR EMAIL DELIVERY

There are two timing details that you may want to keep in mind regarding the delivery of your emails: 1) time of day and 2) amount of time between emails. For the time of day, try to avoid sending emails outside of the standard business hours where the email might become part of a long list of unread emails that the prospect sees when they start their day as that can increase the odds of an instant delete. Try to send your email when there is a good chance that the prospect is at his or her desk and in the morning between 8 a.m. and 9 a.m. or just after lunch between 1 p.m. and 2 p.m. are good windows of time for this.

The other thing you will want to think about is how much time to leave between the emails you send to each prospect. For cold prospects who do not know who you are, one week between prospecting emails is a good cadence. If you are emailing prospects that know who you are or have engaged with you in some way or another, you could get more aggressive with a couple of days between emails.

GETTING EMAIL ADDRESSES

In order to use an approach where you are sending cold emails, you will need email addresses. For this, you can either buy lists of contacts with email addresses from list brokers or you can subscribe to different contact database services that provide email addresses.

However, you may find yourself coming across contacts where you do not have their email address. In this situation, you can use a process of trying to guess the prospect's email address because most corporate email addresses use one of the below naming convention formats for their company email addresses:

- [first name].[last name]@websiteaddress.com
- [first letter of first name][last name]@websiteaddress.com
- [first name]_[last name]@websiteaddress.com
- [first name]@websiteaddress.com
- [first name][last name]@websiteaddress.com
- [first name][first letter of last name]@websiteaddress.com

If you have the prospect's name and you know their company's website address, you have what you need to guess the email address using these common formats. If you try to guess the email address and your guess is incorrect, you will usually receive an email back saying your email attempt was undeliverable. If you receive an undeliverable message, you can try again with a different format and usually after a few guesses, you will find a combination that does not create an undeliverable response.

While this process works about 80 percent of the time, it is a little tedious. The SalesScripter software application actually solves that problem as it provides a tool called Email Guesser that does all of this work for you. If you enter the three values of first name, last name, and company website address, the software will create all of the different combinations and send a test ping for each one and then tell you which combination is a good email address for the contact.

CHAPTER 19

Voicemail Strategy

When you cold call prospects, a major portion of your calls will go to voicemail boxes. With that being such a likely outcome, it is important to use some sort of logic or strategy for what to do (and not do) when you get a prospect's voicemail box, and that is provided in this chapter.

Start with Trying to Understand the Prospect

In order to figure out what to do with the prospect's voicemail box, it helps to start out by trying to understand the prospect.

PROSPECTS ARE OFTEN AWAY FROM THEIR DESKS

When you call a prospect multiple times and every call goes to his or her voicemail box, you may think that the prospect is avoiding your call. But the reality is that if you are calling a decision maker, he or she is likely extremely busy and can be away in meetings most of the day or completely out of the office traveling for multiple days at a time. It is very possible that the prospect is never at his or her desk, and this is why you keep getting the voicemail box.

PROSPECTS GET A LOT OF CALLS FROM SALESPEOPLE

Decision makers get so many calls from salespeople that their phones will ring all day. With that, if they are away from their desks for an extended period of time, their voice-mail boxes will often fill up with messages from salespeople.

PROSPECTS WILL NOT LISTEN TO MANY OF THE MESSAGES

For prospects who get a lot of voicemail messages, it is very likely that they will not listen to every message due to the sheer volume of messages that are being left every day.

PROSPECTS DO NOT CALL SALESPEOPLE BACK

Salespeople often complain about prospects not returning their calls after they leave voicemail messages, and they ponder what to say to get prospects to call back. It is not good to spend time and energy thinking about this because it is my belief that prospects do not return calls from voicemails that are left by salespeople. This might sound a bit pessimistic, but I base this assumption on the following factors:

- The prospect is too busy to return the call.
- The prospect is not interested (yet).
- The prospect has a certain level of ego and feels it is below him or her to call a salesperson back.
- The prospect assumes the salesperson will call back again.
- The prospect intends to call the salesperson back but forgets to.
- The prospect does not listen to the message.

All of these points about understanding the prospect may sound a bit negative and that I am trying to talk you out of calling the prospect all together. That is not the point of this exercise. More so, the goal here is to better understand the prospect and be able to picture what is going on with that person so that you can make better decisions regarding your voicemail messages.

Tips for Your Voicemail Strategy

Here are some tips for your voicemail messages.

WHETHER OR NOT TO LEAVE A VOICEMAIL

Even though the prospect might not listen to your voicemail message or return your call, I believe you should still leave a message because it is one of your options for trying to communicate with the prospect. Not a great option, but one of the few options you have, so you might as well use it and leave messages at certain times.

WHEN TO LEAVE MESSAGES

While you should leave voicemail messages, you do not want to leave one on every call attempt because there are some advantages to hanging up with no message:

- It takes time to leave voicemail messages, and that can be saved by hanging up.
- You can make more calls overall with the time you saved.
- You can call the prospect back sooner if you don't leave a message.

The logic with the third point is that if I leave a voicemail message, I need to wait at least a few days before I call back again. But if I hang up without leaving a voicemail message, I can call back the next day or even the same day as I can assume the prospect does not know I called earlier and I am just trying to call again.

With that, my suggestion is to primarily call without leaving voicemail messages, but at certain intervals change that approach to leave voicemail messages. The logic is that you are using the voicemail box periodically to deliver your sales message, but for the most part, you are calling with no message so that you can move quicker and be able to call the prospect more frequently.

FOCUS THE MESSAGE ON THE RIGHT GOAL

Most salespeople will leave voicemail messages with the main goal of trying to get the prospect to call them back. But if we agree that the prospect has a low probability of returning the call, then maybe we should not structure the message around the goal of getting the prospect to call back. In other words, if you have twenty seconds of time to leave a message, why spend it asking the prospect to do something that person is not likely to do?

Another way to go is to focus your message around the goal of trying to educate the prospect about who you are, how you can help, and why he or she might want to talk with you the next time you call.

WHAT TO SAY IN YOUR MESSAGE

If you know that you might have to call the prospect multiple times and might have to leave multiple voicemails, you can break your sales message down and share part of it each time you leave a message. This will allow you educate the prospect on who you are each time you leave a message.

One way to do this is to share a different building block on each voicemail message that you leave. For example, on your first voicemail message, you could leave a message that shares some of your value points. On your next voice mail message, you can share some of your pain points. On the third message, you can share your name-drop example. And if you need to leave a fourth voicemail message, you can share some details about your product.

CHANGE YOUR EXPECTATIONS

When you leave a bunch of voicemail messages and nobody calls you back, you can feel bad and that you are not doing your job well. But when you realize that prospects don't call salespeople back, you can start to have a better mindset by realizing that you are not doing anything wrong and this is just part of the process.

This is basically a shift in expectations where you go from waiting for prospects to call you back to having more clarity about what is actually going on. This can not only help you to stay more positive and focused on what you need to do to continue to pursue and get a hold of prospects, but it can also improve your decision-making by preventing you from prematurely labeling prospects as uninterested based primarily on the fact that they did not return your voicemail messages.

DO NOT ASK THE PROSPECT TO CALL YOU BACK

Instead of asking for a call back, tell the prospect that you are going to call back. I say this for a couple of reasons:

- **It is rude:** If you ask a prospect to call you back in a voicemail message, you are asking them to perform a task, and I believe this is rude at this point in the sales process. You are the one that is trying to start the conversation and earn the prospect's attention and business. While you can certainly ask the prospect to perform certain tasks later in the sales process, it is your job to spend the energy and effort to get connected at the very beginning of the sales process.

- **You keep control:** This change means that you will keep ownership and control over the next callback. Yes, it would be great to have the prospect call you back, but by keeping control of that task, you can make sure it happens.

Also, telling the prospect you are going to call back lets the prospect know that you are going to keep reaching out. This could motivate the prospect to answer your call, respond to one of your emails, or call you back because the prospect will think that he or she has to engage with you at some point due to your persistence.

SEND A VOICEMAIL FOLLOW-UP EMAIL

After you leave a voicemail message for a prospect, follow that up with an email for these four reasons:

1. **Reinforces your message:** If you leave a voicemail message with some of your value points and then you send a voicemail follow-up email with the same value points, you are reinforcing the message you are trying to deliver, and this can increase the odds that your message gets received.

2. **Easier to respond to:** It is technically easier for a prospect to reply to an email than to return a call from a voicemail message. With that, you can increase the probability of a response to your voicemail message if you provide a response option that is easier for the prospect.

3. **Easier to extract contact info:** It is much easier for the prospect to get your contact information from an email signature than trying to write it down while listening to a voicemail message.

4. **Easier to file away:** If your prospect wants to save your information for a later date, it is much easier for him or her to save an email than it is to save a voicemail message.

Applying the Tips to a Voicemail Message

Here is a voicemail message that takes all of those tips into consideration.

VOICEMAIL MESSAGE – VALUE POINTS

Hello [Prospect Name], this is [Your Name] with [Your Company].

The reason for my call is that we help [Target Buyer Type] to:

(Share 1 to 3 value points)

- *Value Point 1*
- *Value Point 2*
- *Value Point 3*

I actually don't know if you are interested in improving those areas and that is why I am reaching out.

I will try you again next week. If you would like to reach me in the meantime, my number is [Your Number].

Again, this is [Your Name] calling from [Your Company], [Your Number Again].

Thank you and I look forward to talking with you soon.

Explanation

- **Share one to three value points:** You can share just one value point, two, or three. The main factor that impacts how many you share is how long your individual value points are. If they are long sentences, you probably should only share one point. If they are just a couple of words, you could share more than one.

- **Sales takeaway:** There is a soft sales takeaway after the benefits, and this is optional. It makes the message a little longer, but it adds a nice touch by disarming the prospect and can make you sound more consultative.

But this statement is totally optional, and you can leave it out if you prefer.

- **Doesn't ask for callback:** Instead of asking the prospect to call back, this message says that you will be calling again next week. But even though you are taking ownership of the callback task, the message still leaves your phone number in case the prospect would like to perform the callback task. This lets the prospect know that you are going to do all of the work and continue to own the task of calling back. It also lets the prospect know that you are going to keep trying to get a hold of him or her, and this could motivate the prospect to answer your next call or reply to your voicemail follow-up email.

- **Sharing your contact info:** It is good to leave your contact info twice so that it is easier for the contact to hear your contact details in the event that the prospect decides to write your information down.

VOICEMAIL FOLLOW-UP EMAIL - VALUE POINTS

Here is an example of a follow-up email that is paired with the example voicemail message:

Subject Line: Following Up My Voicemail - [Your Company]

Hello [Contact First Name],

As I mentioned in a voicemail I just left you, we help [Target Buyer Type] to:

- Value Point 1
- Value Point 2
- Value Point 3

I don't know if you want to improve those areas and that is why I am reaching out.

Are you available for a brief 15 to 20 minute meeting where I can share some examples of how we have helped other [Target Buyer Type] to [Value Point]?

Best Regards,
[Email Signature]

CHAPTER 20

Getting into New Accounts

If you are a B2B salesperson, one of your biggest challenges will be getting prospects on the phone. You can have the best product, the best price, and the best sales pitch, but if you can't get in front of the customer, having all of those great things will not do you any good.

While there is nothing you can do to get prospects to physically pick up the phone when you call, there are three things that you can do to improve your connect rate:

1. Prospecting Cadence
2. Organizational Movement
3. Concentrated Prospecting

Prospecting Cadence

A common question that salespeople ask is how many times to call a prospect. While it is difficult to say that you should call prospects X number of times because every situation is unique, we can say that in most cases, you are probably not calling prospects enough. If you called a prospect five times and left one voicemail message, you might feel like you are being a pest and that the prospect must be not interested since he or she did not answer and did not call you back. But the reality is that the prospect could have been away from his or her desk every time that you called and did not listen to your voicemail message.

In this hypothetical scenario, you need to continue to reach out to this prospect with a schedule of call attempts and also try to reach out with different types of communication methods. That process of contacting the prospect multiple times and in different ways is what I refer to as your prospecting cadence, and I will give you some ideas for how to build your cadence next.

CADENCE EXAMPLE

Cadence is synonymous with rhythm. And just like how rhythm is the frequency or tempo that a musician might hit different notes, your prospecting cadence is the rhythm, frequency, or tempo that you can use for how often you contact the prospect, the methods you use for reaching out, and what you say in your messages.

We just finished talking about cold calling, email prospecting, and voicemail messages. You can use each of those as the main elements of your prospecting cadence. You can certainly also include other communication methods like social media, direct mail, cold walking, etc.

With just focusing on calls, emails, and voicemails, here is an example of a prospecting cadence workflow:

Round 1
Round 1 starts with a cold email.

> **Day 1:** Send a cold email to the prospect. For this example, we will use the cold email with the value points building block for the first round.

> **Day 2 through 7:** During the next few days, you can call the prospect one to five times without leaving a voicemail message.

> **Day 8:** On the next call attempt, leave the value points voicemail message and send the prospect the voicemail follow-up email that aligns with the value points voicemail message.

> **Days 9 through 14:** After you leave a voicemail message, pause your attempts to contact the prospect for a period of one week.

That will complete Round 1 of the prospecting cadence.

Round 2

Repeat the exact same process but try to use different messages for your emails and voicemail.

> **Day 15:** Send a cold email to the prospect. You can use the cold email with the pain points building block for the second round.
>
> **Day 16 through 21:** During the next few days, you can call the prospect one to five times without leaving a voicemail message.
>
> **Day 22:** On the next call attempt, leave the pain points voicemail message and send the prospect the voicemail follow-up email that aligns with the pain points voicemail message.
>
> **Days 23 through 28:** Pause contact attempts.

That will complete Round 2 of the prospecting cadence.

Round 3

Repeat the exact same process but try to use different messages for your emails and voicemail.

> **Day 29:** Send a cold email to the prospect. You can use the cold email with the name-drop building block for the third round.
>
> **Day 30 through 35:** During the next few days, you can call the prospect one to five times without leaving a voicemail message.
>
> **Day 36:** On the next call attempt, leave the name-drop voicemail message and send the prospect the voicemail follow-up email that aligns with the name-drop voicemail message.

Days 37 through 42: Pause contact attempts.

That will complete Round 3 of the prospecting cadence.

Round 4
Repeat the exact same process but try to use different messages for your emails and voicemail.

Day 43: Send a cold email to the prospect. You can use the cold email with the product building block for the fourth round.

Day 44 through 49: During the next few days, you can call the prospect one to five times without leaving a voicemail message.

Day 50: On the next call attempt, leave the product voicemail message and send the prospect the voicemail follow-up email that aligns with the product voicemail message.

Days 51: Pause contact attempts indefinitely.

At the end of Round 4, if you still have not been able to get a hold of the prospect, you can mark them as unreachable and move on to spend your valuable time pursuing other prospects.

Here is what this prospecting cadence looks like on a calendar.

Sunday	Monday	Tuesday	Wednesday	Thursday	Friday	Saturday
	1 Round 1 Cold Email	2 Call Attempt – No Voicemail	3 Call Attempt – No Voicemail	4 Call Attempt – No Voicemail	5 Call Attempt – No Voicemail	6 Call Attempt – No Voicemail
7 Call Attempt – No Voicemail	8 Call Attempt – With Voicemail Send Voicemail Follow-Up Email	9 Pause	10 Pause	11 Pause	12 Pause	13 Pause
14 Pause	15 Round 2 Cold Email #2	16 Call Attempt – No Voicemail	17 Call Attempt – No Voicemail	18 Call Attempt – No Voicemail	19 Call Attempt – No Voicemail	20 Call Attempt – No Voicemail
21 Call Attempt – No Voicemail	22 Call Attempt – With Voicemail Send Voicemail Follow-Up Email	23 Pause	24 Pause	25 Pause	26 Pause	27 Pause
28 Pause	29 Round 3 Cold Email #3	30 Call Attempt – No Voicemail	31 Call Attempt – No Voicemail	32 Call Attempt – No Voicemail	33 Call Attempt – No Voicemail	34 Call Attempt – No Voicemail
35 Call Attempt – No Voicemail	36 Call Attempt – With Voicemail Send Voicemail Follow-Up Email	37 Pause	38 Pause	39 Pause	40 Pause	41 Pause
42 Pause	43 Round 4 Cold Email #4	44 Call Attempt – No Voicemail	45 Call Attempt – No Voicemail	46 Call Attempt – No Voicemail	47 Call Attempt – No Voicemail	48 Call Attempt – No Voicemail
49 Call Attempt – No Voicemail	50 Call Attempt – With Voicemail Send Voicemail Follow-Up Email					

You can follow the prospecting cadence workflow with the steps that we outlined, or you can use this structure to get ideas in order to build your own cadence. You can build off of this by using different messages, modifying the timing and number of contact attempts, and adding additional contact methods. And whether you use our workflow or use your own, it is not critical that you follow it exactly, making each call on the exact day specified by the cadence. The key thing here is to use some sort of process to help you to make sure you have a persistent effort in your pursuit to get connected with prospects.

Organizational Movement

If you are trying to get your foot in the door of an account and the target prospect never answers his or her phone, this will seem like a significant barrier preventing you from selling to that account. The simple workaround for this is to find other contacts at the account that you can call in order to find another way in. Sure, the other people may be difficult to get a hold of also, but if you increase the number of contacts you are calling from one to three, you increase the odds that you end up talking to someone.

We refer to this process of finding other people at an account as organizational movement, and there are two different types of movement:

Vertical Movement

This is moving up and down the different levels of the department for your target prospect to find new contacts. For example, if your target prospect is the director of finance and you can't get a hold of that person, you can move up the organization to try to contact the VP of finance. You can also move down the organization to try to contact the finance manager.

Horizontal Movement

This is moving laterally to find contacts in other functional departments. For example, if you are calling the director of finance and can't get a hold of that person, you can move horizontally to contact people at the same level in other departments, like the director of IT, the director of operations, the director of human resources, etc.

A good tool to use for organizational movement is LinkedIn as it makes it easy to find different contacts at the account that you are trying to get into. Simply go to LinkedIn and perform a search with the company name to find other contacts to pursue.

COMBINING CADENCE WITH MOVEMENT

Getting a hold of prospects is tough, but when you combine prospecting cadence with organizational movement, you greatly improve your ability to get into new accounts. The way to combine these concepts is that when you reach the end of Round 2 in your prospecting cadence, you can then apply either horizontal or vertical movement to find another contact at the account. When you find a new contact to pursue, start this person at the beginning of your prospecting cadence workflow. With this added step, you will now have two people you are pursuing at the account, and this will increase your odds of getting in.

Concentrated Prospecting

A third tactic that you can consider implementing is concentrated prospecting, and this is to focus your prospecting on a small set of contacts or accounts. For example, if you have a list of five hundred contacts, applying concentrated prospecting would be to take twenty-five or fifty contacts from the list and only focus on that short list. As you remove contacts from the list by classifying as either disqualified or unreachable, you can then refill those spots with contacts from the master list.

I first started thinking about this when I had a salesperson working for me and I gave her a list of five hundred contacts to cold call. She was an excellent salesperson, but she had very poor results with this project, and I started to look at what she was doing and noticed that she started at the top of the list and called each prospect once and then moved on to the next as she worked her way to the bottom of the list. After a couple of weeks and barely talking to anyone, I started to think the problem was the way that she was working the list. Since prospects are difficult to get a hold of and are often away from their desks, she needed more call attempts in order to increase the odds of catching them. With that, I made one small change, and that was that I took fifty contacts from the list of five hundred, and told her to focus only on those and that I would give her more when she was able disqualify contacts from the list. By focusing on a smaller number of target contacts, she increased the number of attempts per contact, and this immediately increased her connect rate and the number of leads that she was able to generate.

If you are working a list of contacts, a good target contact list size is between twenty-five to fifty. If you are working a list of accounts, I cannot tell you what number of target accounts is best because it can vary depending on the size of organization. For example, if you are calling small businesses, your target account list could be twenty-five, fifty, or one hundred. But if you are calling large organizations, you target account list could be five, ten, or twenty.

CHAPTER 21

Dealing with Objections

You are likely to face objections on almost every cold call that you make. With that, if you can simply become a little more prepared for the objections that are likely to come up, you will immediately make your sales efforts both easier and more successful. In this chapter, we will provide a very easy to adopt process that you can use for dealing with and getting around the objections that you will face when prospecting.

Common Objections

Here are some of the most common objections that you might have to face:

- *I do not have time right now.*
- *What is this in regards to?*
- *Is this a sales call?*
- *I am not interested.*
- *We do not have budget/money to spend right now.*
- *We already use someone for that.*
- *We are not making any changes right now.*
- *Just send me your information.*
- *Call me back in X months.*

These will come up again and again, so it will help you tremendously to take a little time to think about how to respond to these and then have those responses ready to go when you are making calls. If you read those objections and don't know what you should say, do not worry as we will provide you with tips on how to respond to all of these in this chapter.

Some Things to Keep in Mind

Here are a few things to keep in mind regarding objections and how you should respond to them.

THE GOAL IS TO KEEP THE CONVERSATION GOING

When you get an objection, your natural instinct is to try to resolve the objection. For example, if the prospect tells you that he or she is not interested, your reflexive response is to say something to try to make the prospect interested. I want you to resist this natural instinct and focus more on simply trying to keep the conversation going.

UNDERSTAND THE PROSPECT

In order to improve your ability to deal with objections, first try to understand why prospects use objections.

- **They want to get rid of you:** Your call might be a disruption, and they simply want to get rid of you so that they can get back to what you are distracting them from.

- **They think you are a salesperson:** They sense that you are a salesperson who is trying to sell something, and this triggers an instinct to try to get rid of you.

- **They think they do not need what you are selling:** They may truly believe that they do not need what you sell.

- **They are not in buying mode:** They are not in buying mode for what you sell.

If those are valid reasons why a prospect might use objections, these can help us to figure out how best to respond and how to adjust the approach to trigger less objections all together.

DON'T SOUND LIKE A SALESPERSON

When you look at the reasons why a prospect might use objections, you can see how important it is to not look like a salesperson who is trying to sell something. Decreasing the amount to which you look like a salesperson will decrease the amount of objections and resistance that you face.

DON'T SELL THE PRODUCT, SELL THE MEETING

Most objections are trying to stop the ultimate goal of you trying to sell your product. For example, all of these objections are the prospect telling you that he or she does not want to buy your product:

- *I am not interested.*
- *We already use someone for that.*
- *We are not making any changes right now.*
- *We do not have budget/money to spend right now.*

But if your goal is not to sell the product, these objections actually become invalid. The fact that the prospect already uses someone today is a valid reason to not buy your product today, but it is not a valid reason to end the conversation. The fact that the prospect does not have budget is a valid reason to not buy from you today, but it is not a valid reason to end a conversation.

DISARM AND EDUCATE

If a prospect gives you an objection that is blocking your ultimate goal of trying to sell your product, you can try to disarm the prospect by explaining that you are not trying to sell anything by saying something like this at the very beginning of your objection response:

> *I understand. And I want you to know that I am actually not trying to sell you anything or sign you up for anything at this point.*

> *I don't even know if you are a good fit with what we provide.*

This is not only designed to disarm the prospect, but it is also designed to coach the prospect on the process that you are trying to take them through, which is to simply have a conversation.

Options for Handling Objections

You have three main options for how to handle objections: 1) comply, 2) overcome, or 3) deflect.

OPTION 1: COMPLY WITH THE OBJECTION

To comply with an objection is to accept it and here is an example:

> **Prospect:** *I am not interested.*

> **Salesperson:** *OK, I understand. Have a nice day.*

There are moments where you will need to comply and accept the prospect's objection. But the key is knowing when to comply and when not to. You have probably heard the saying "Don't take no for an answer." I would like to change that to "Know when to take no for an answer," and here are two simple rules for that:

1. Don't comply and accept the objection until you have tried to get around the objection at least three times.

2. Comply and accept the objection if it is a true showstopper in terms of the prospect completely not fitting with what you sell. For example, if you sell lawn care services and the prospect does not own a home or have a lawn, you can comply with this objection.

OPTION 2: OVERCOME THE OBJECTION

To overcome the objection would be to try to resolve the objection or change the prospect's mind, and here is an example:

Prospect: *I am not interested.*

Salesperson: *OK, but we usually increase sales between 25 to 30 percent. You are not interested in that type of growth?*

To try to overcome an objection is fairly difficult because you are basically trying to change the prospect's mind. While this is doable and something you have to do when selling, it is fairly difficult to change the prospect's mind regarding an objection during the Initial Contact sales process step for these three reasons:

1. The Initial Contact sales process step will usually be a very brief call or conversation, and you will not have the time and attention needed to explain your case for why the prospect should change his or her mind.

2. When the prospect is giving an objection because he or she does not want to buy your product, you do not need to change the prospect's mind and overcome this objection because your goal is not to sell the product at the Initial Contact sales step.

3. When you try to overcome an objection, this can put more attention on it, giving the objection more life and energy in the prospect's mind.

But it is important to keep in mind that all of those points apply to the Initial Contact sales process step. Once you are beyond that and in the Meeting or the Presentation, trying to overcome objections is certainly more of an option for you because you will have more time, attention, and rapport with the prospect. This will put you in a better position to try to present your case as to why the prospect should change his or her mind.

OPTION 3: DEFLECT THE OBJECTION

The third option is to deflect the objection, and this is to try to let the objection bounce off of you in order to keep the conversation going. Here is an example:

Prospect: *I am not interested.*

Salesperson: *I understand. Do you mind if I ask how long it takes you for reconciliation?*

The way the deflect response works is that you might acknowledge the objection by saying something like "I understand" or "Oh, OK." You can then deflect by following that with a question. In many cases, your prospect will respond to the question you ask, and you then have three different directions to go:

1. You can ask a follow-up question to inquire more about the prospect's answer to your first question.

2. You can ask a different question to keep the conversation going and learn more.

3. You can try to close the prospect on the next sales process step based on the prospect's answer.

Your pain and current environment questions will usually be great questions to ask when trying to deflect objections. You can also deflect to your pain points and to your sales process, and we will show you what all of these deflections look like in the next section.

Deflecting Objections

Here are some ways to deflect the objections we outlined earlier.

I do not have time.

This is a very common objection when cold calling, and a very simple response to this can be:

> Oh, I understand. I can be very brief, or I can call you back at another time. Which would you prefer?

or

> Oh, OK. What is the best time for me to call you back?

With this response, if the prospect is truly not too busy for your call, he or she may just end up giving you a couple of minutes when you suggest calling back again at another time.

What is this in regards to?

This is the main "go to" objection for gatekeepers and prospects because it is very effective at identifying if the person calling is a salesperson who is trying to sell something. Since you are a salesperson who is trying to sell something, if you comply with this objection, you might say something like:

- I am calling to introduce myself.
- I am calling to introduce our company.
- I am calling to see if you need our services.
- I am calling to schedule a meeting.

And if your answer is close to any of those, the gatekeeper or prospect will likely try to get rid of you with another objection. I am not suggesting that you be dishonest or misrepresent who you are, but you can avoid answering the question directly and stay in the game a little longer by responding with your value points building block with something like this:

Value Points

Well, the reason for my call is that we help [Target Buyer Type] to:

- *Value Point 1*
- *Value Point 2*
- *Value Point 3*

I am not saying that the prospect or gatekeeper will hear this response and completely drop his or her guardedness. More so, it is designed to throw the other person off by not giving an answer that confirms you are a salesperson who is trying to sell something. After you share this objection response with your value points, just sit there and wait for the other person to speak as he or she will likely respond by either asking another question, giving a different objection, transferring you to the prospect, or letting you start a conversation. If the person asks another question or gives you a different objection, you have successfully gotten around the initial objection and can deal with the new question or objection.

The other good thing about using your value points for deflecting objections is that since your value points are usually very positive improvements that your product offers, it is difficult for gatekeepers and prospects to respond that they are not interested. For example, if your value is that you make people happier, it is difficult for a prospect to respond to that he or she is not interested in being happier.

Is this a sales call?
You can respond to this objection with the exact same response as the "What is this call in regards to?" objection.

Value Points

Well, the reason for my call is that we help [Target Buyer Type] to:

- *Value Point 1*
- *Value Point 2*
- *Value Point 3*

I am not interested.
You need to prepare for this objection because it will come up very frequently. Remember, the fact that the prospect is not interested is a valid reason to not purchase your product, but it is not a valid reason to end the conversation. With that, try to keep the conversation going by deflecting to either your pain questions or pain points, and that could look like this:

Option 1: Pain Questions

I understand. Do you mind if I ask real quick:

- *Pain Question 1*
- *Pain Question 2*
- *Pain Question 3*

Option 2: Pain Points

I understand. When I talk with other [Target Buyer Type], they often have challenges with:

- *Pain Point 1*
- *Pain Point 2*
- *Pain Point 3*

Are you are concerned about any of those areas?

Just send me your information.

This is one of the most common objections that gatekeepers and prospects use because it is a very effective way to end the call without being rude. While sometimes they may genuinely want your information, most of the time they are just blowing you off. The worst thing you could probably do is interpret this request for information as genuine interest and then spend twenty minutes putting together an email that has a very nice summary of your information, all of which may go straight to the trash when it is received.

Regardless of whether or not the request for information is genuine, you can deflect this objection with your pain or current environment questions to keep the call going and extract more information.

Option 1: Pain Questions

Sure, I can definitely do that. So that I know what best to send you, can I ask you real quick:

- *Pain Question 1*
- *Pain Question 2*
- *Pain Question 3*

Option 2: Current Environment Questions

Sure, I can definitely do that. So that I know what best to send you, can I ask you real quick:

- *Who are you currently using today?*
- *How long have you been with them?*
- *How is everything going?*
- *What are some things you like about what they provide?*
- *What are some things that you think could be better?*
- *If you could change one thing about their product/service, what would it be?*
- *When was the last time you considered other options in this area?*
- *(Sizing Question) How many _____ do you currently have?*
- *Are you the right person to discuss this area with?*

There will be times where the "Just send me your information" objection comes up at the end of a call, and this is more of a hesitation on moving forward to the next step in your sales process rather than the prospect trying to blow you off. In this scenario, you may have already asked a lot of your questions, so an alternative option for you is to deflect to your sales process by suggesting that it might make more sense to meet instead of sending over a lot of information with the response below.

Option 3: Sales Process

> *Sure, I definitely can. Actually, there is a lot of information that I can send over to you. If you have questions about something in particular, it might be easier and quicker to have a brief conversation over the phone on another day instead of me sending over a bunch of information.*

We already use someone/something today for that.

It is very likely that the prospect already uses (or has) what you are trying to sell. And while that is a valid reason for him or her to not purchase from you today, it is not a valid reason to end the conversation. With that, you can deflect this objection with your current environment questions, pain questions, or pain points in your attempt to keep the conversation going.

Option 1: Current Environment Questions

Oh, great.

- *Who are you currently using today?*
- *How long have you been with them?*
- *How is everything going?*
- *What are some things you like about what they provide?*
- *What are some things that you think could be better?*
- *If you could change one thing about their product/service, what would it be?*
- *When was the last time you considered other options in this area?*
- *(Sizing Question) How many _____ do you currently have?*
- *Are you the right person to discuss this area with?*

Option 2: Pain Questions

Oh, great. Do you mind if I ask real quick:

- *Pain Question 1*
- *Pain Question 2*
- *Pain Question 3*

Option 3: Pain Points

Oh, great. When I talk with other [Target Buyer Type], they often have challenges with:

- *Pain Point 1*
- *Pain Point 2*
- *Pain Point 3*

Are you are concerned about any of those areas?

I do not have budget/money.

The fact that the prospect does not have budget is a valid reason to not purchase what you sell today, but it is not a valid reason to end the conversation. You could try to explain this by deflecting to your sales process by focusing on trying to sell the meeting with the response below.

Option 1: Sales Process

> *I understand. And I want you to know that I am not reaching out to you to try to sign you up or sell you anything. More so, we are just looking to open the dialogue between our two companies and have an initial conversation.*

> *We would like to learn a little more about you and possibly share some information about us. That way, when you begin your budget planning or when your budget opens back up, you can know who we are and how we can help.*

> *Are you open to having a brief conversation at some point? It does not have to be this week or next, we are not going anywhere.*

You can also respond to this objection by deflecting with your pain questions or your pain points.

Option 2: Pain Questions

> *I understand. Do you mind if I ask real quick:*

> * *Pain Question 1*
> * *Pain Question 2*

211

- *Pain Question 3*

Option 3: Pain Points

I understand. When I talk with other [Target Buyer Type], they often have challenges with:

- *Pain Point 1*
- *Pain Point 2*
- *Pain Point 3*

Are you are concerned about any of those areas?

We are not looking to make any changes right now.

You can respond to this objection by deflecting with your pain questions, pain points, or current environment questions.

Option 1: Pain Questions

I understand. Do you mind if I ask real quick:

- *Pain Question 1*
- *Pain Question 2*
- *Pain Question 3*

Option 2: Current Environment Questions

I understand.

- *Who are you currently using today?*
- *How long have you been with them?*

- *How is everything going?*
- *What are some things you like about what they provide?*
- *What are some things that you think could be better?*
- *If you could change one thing about their product/service, what would it be?*
- *When was the last time you considered other options in this area?*
- *(Sizing Question) How many _____ do you currently have?*
- *Are you the right person to discuss this area with?*

Option 3: Pain Points

I understand. When I talk with other [Target Buyer Type], they often have challenges with:

- *Pain Point 1*
- *Pain Point 2*
- *Pain Point 3*

Are you are concerned about any of those areas?

But another option you have is to deflect with your sales process with something like:

Option 4: Sales Process

I understand. And I want you to know that I am not reaching out to you to try to sign you up or sell you anything. More so, we are just looking to open the dialogue between our two companies and have an initial conversation.

We would like to learn a little more about you and possibly share some information about us. That way, when you ready to make a change, you can know who we are and how we can help.

Are you open to having a brief conversation at some point? It does not have to be this week or next, we are not going anywhere.

Call me back in X months.

Sometimes a prospect will tell you to call back in a certain number of months. He or she may do this to try to get rid of you without being rude, or there may be a legitimate reason why that point in time would be a better time to talk. But since you are selling the meeting and not selling the product, this is not a valid reason to end the conversation, and you can explain that with this response below.

Option 1: Sales Process

I can certainly do that. But I want you to know that I am not reaching out to you to try to sign you up or sell you anything. More so, we are just looking to open the dialogue between our two companies and have an initial conversation.

We would like to learn a little more about you and possibly share some information about us. That way, when you ready to look closer at this, you can know who we are and how we can help.

Are you open to having a brief conversation at some point? It does not have to be this week or next, we are not going anywhere.

If you have already met with the prospect and you are deeper into the sales process, you could use any information that you have gathered on the prospect's pain points and challenges with a pain points response that could look something like this:

Option 2: Customer Specific Pain Points

I can certainly do that. But when we last spoke, you mentioned you had challenges with:

- *Customer Concern 1*
- *Customer Concern 2*
- *Customer Concern 3*

Are you sure it makes sense to put off talking another X months with those going on?

Overcoming Objections

If you are at the Meeting or Presentation sales process steps or beyond, you might want to try to overcome objections. It is difficult to tell you what to say or do to overcome objections because there are so many different scenarios, and every product is different. But here are a couple of steps to consider when trying to overcome objections.

Step 1—Get to the root: Try to understand why the prospect is giving you the objection. For example, if the prospect says that your product is too expensive, you can dig deeper to try to find out what he or she means by that or what is driving that concern. Is the prospect saying this because he or she does not have enough money to spend? Or is the prospect looking at competitors that have a lower price? Or is it that the prospect does not see or understand the value that your product offers? Once you understand the root of the objection, you will be in a better position to figure out how to respond and what to do.

Step 2—Capture the full picture: The next step is to try to capture the full picture in terms of other details that are related to the prospect's objection. In other words, try to find out other things that are impacting or related to the prospect's position. For example, if your prospect says he or she cannot afford your product, you could try to uncover some of the other costs that are related to your product in order to see the full picture of what is going on. One way this could help you is that you might be able to identify costs that you can make go away with the purchase of your product. In other words, you could overcome the objection that the prospect cannot afford your product by finding ways to decrease costs in other areas.

Step 3—Present your case: The next step is to present your case. For example, if your price is higher but the total cost of ownership is less when factoring in other costs, then you need to explain this and educate the prospect in order to try to overcome the objection.

Step 4—Identify if it is a showstopper: At some point, it is important to identify if there is an agreement to keep moving forward or if the concern is a legitimate reason to stop discussions. Don't be afraid to close the file and walk away if the prospect's objection is tied to a legitimate reason why he or she will not be able to buy your product as it will likely be a problem when it is time to close the deal, and you could stand to lose all of the valuable time that you spent working with the prospect.

Create an Objections Map

Create a document that lists out your anticipated objections and have a couple of options for how to respond to each objection. Once you have this document, there are three different ways you can use this sales tool:

1. **Review the objections map before you make calls.** Scan over your objections map before you make calls so that your responses are fresh in your mind.

2. **Use as a guide when on a call.** Have your objections map in front of you and use it as a guide when on a call. Since calls are extremely fast-paced, try to be familiar with the objections and responses and just use the objections map more as a reminder of what you need to say.

3. **Use as a training tool after your calls end.** You can also use your objections map after a call ends to compare what you said with what is on the objections map.

REFLECT BACK TO IMPROVE MOVING FORWARD

There is something to learn from almost every call that you make. With that, I recommend a process of reflecting back after a call ends to think about what just happened so that you can be better prepared the next time that same situation happens. Here are a few things to try to think about when reflecting back on a call:

What went well: After a call ends, try to think about what went well. This is helpful to not only maintain a strong mental mindset, but it is also good to think about the things you did well so that you remember to do them again.

What could have gone better: Try to think about what did not go well and what you could have done better if you could go back or if you found yourself in the same exact situation again. This will greatly increase the chances of you handling that situation better on future calls.

What objections came up: Identify what objection you had to face during the call. This might be a good time to look at the objections map to see if the objection is on there. If it is not, you may want to add it so that you can be more prepared for that objection the next time it comes up.

How you responded to the objection: Try to remember what you said when your prospect gave you the objection. Did your response do a good job of keeping the call going? Try to think about how the prospect responded to what you said and think about anything you could have done differently so that you can improve how you handle the same objection next time. This is a good time to make any changes or additions to your objections map as this will help to make the document a more helpful and valuable sales tool.

Questions you could you have asked: Cold calls can be very quick and go in many different directions. With that, it can often be hard to always think of the right questions to ask. Sometimes after a call ends and you have more time to digest what the prospect said, you can think of questions that would have been good to ask to either keep the call going or extract more information from the prospect. And while this does not do you much good with the call that just ended, the same situations repeat again and again, and this process will help you get better at asking good questions on future calls.

CHAPTER 22

Getting Around Gatekeepers

When performing B2B cold calling, you can spend 50 percent or more of your time dealing with gatekeepers. With that being such a large percentage, improving your ability to get around gatekeepers can have a big impact on your level of success. In this chapter, I will provide you with some practical tips and objection responses that will not only help you to get around gatekeepers, but also decrease the frustration and anxiety that you feel while cold calling.

Gatekeepers Tips and Tactics

Here are some tips and tactics that can improve the interactions you have with gatekeepers.

UNDERSTAND THE GATEKEEPER

One of the reasons that gatekeepers can sometimes be difficult and unpleasant is that they are sometimes instructed to keep salespeople out. Gatekeepers are often trained on how to identify when calls are from salespeople who are trying to sell something and how to keep them from getting through to prospects. In many situations, the gatekeeper can actually get in trouble or look bad when salespeople slip past them.

DON'T SOUND LIKE A SALESPERSON

Since many gatekeepers will be instructed to keep salespeople out, you can decrease the level of difficulty that you face by trying to not sound like a salesperson who is trying to sell something. One example of how you can do this is to try to avoid asking the gatekeeper to connect you with someone who makes a particular type of decisions with this type of question:

Can you connect me with the person that makes decisions regarding your website?

This basically tells the gatekeeper that you want to try to sell something that pertains to the website, and it will let the gatekeeper know that he or she needs to be very cautious about letting you in. Try to perform research to find the actual names of people you should to talk to or ask for the title of the person with something like this:

Can you connect me with the director of marketing?

The other area in which you need to be careful about not sounding like a salesperson is how you respond to the gatekeeper's objections, and we will discuss that later in this chapter.

TRY TO ENLIST THEIR HELP

Sometimes you can try to recruit the gatekeeper to help you in your effort to figure out who to talk to. This is not necessarily an option when your gatekeeper is in full "get rid of you" mode as he or she will have zero interest in trying to help you. But when you first start a call with a gatekeeper and have not triggered guardedness, you can try to get the gatekeeper to take more of a helpful role by starting out with one of the statements below:

- *Maybe you can help me with this.*
- *Maybe you can point me in the right direction.*

- *I am not really sure who I need to speak with.*
- *I might need your help with this one.*

Adding your question after that could end up looking something like this:

- *Maybe you can help me with this. I usually work with directors of finance, and I am having trouble finding that person in your organization. Do you know who I should reach out to?*

- *I am not really sure who I need to speak with. I usually work with directors of finance, and I am having trouble finding that person in your organization. Do you know who I should reach out to?*

To improve the odds of this working, try to speak in a way that sounds like a mix of curious and a little lost. If you don't know what this sounds like, try to make the face you would have if you were confused about something when you are talking to the gatekeeper.

TREAT THE GATEKEEPER LIKE THE PROSPECT

If it does not look like the gatekeeper is going to let you through, simply shift gears and start treating the gatekeeper like the target prospect. There are two different ways to do this. First, if the gatekeeper does not understand who you are, who you should talk to, or why the target prospect will want to talk to you, you can try to take a step back and educate the gatekeeper on all of this by sharing either your value points, pain points, or name-drop with something like this:

Value Points

Actually, let me take a step back and let you know why I am calling. The reason for my call is that we help [Target Buyer Type] to:

- *Value Point 1*
- *Value Point 2*
- *Value Point 3*

I don't know if you all want to improve those areas and that is why I am calling. Do you know who the best person for me to talk with is?

Pain Points

Actually, let me take a step back and let you know why I am calling. The reason for my call is that we work with a lot of [Target Buyer Type] and they often have challenges with:

- *Pain Point 1*
- *Pain Point 2*
- *Pain Point 3*

I don't know if you all are concerned about those areas, and that is why I am calling. Do you know who the best person for me to talk with is? Do you know how concerned [Target Prospect] is about these areas?

Name-Drop

Actually, let me take a step back and let you know why I am calling. The reason for my call is that:

- *We worked with [Customer Name] and helped them to [Technical Improvement].*
- *This ultimately helped them to [Business Improvement].*

*I don't know if we can help you in the same way, and that is why I
was calling. Do you know who the best person for me to talk with is?*

The other way that you can treat the gatekeeper like a target prospect is to ask
some of the pain or current environment questions that you were going to ask the
target prospect, and that could look something like this:

Pain Questions

OK. Well, maybe you know the answer to this.

- *Pain Question 1*
- *Pain Question 2*
- *Pain Question 3*

Current Environment Questions

OK. Well, maybe you know the answer to this.

- *Who are you currently using today?*
- *How long have you been with them?*
- *How is everything going?*
- *What are some things you like about what they provide?*
- *What are some things that you think could be better?*
- *If you could change one thing about their product/service, what would it
  be?*
- *When was the last time you considered other options in this area?*
- *(Sizing Question) How many _____ do you currently have?*
- *Are you the right person to discuss this area with?*

If one of the gatekeeper's answers exposes potential pain, you can use that as a
reason to talk with the target prospect with something like this:

Well, that is why it might make sense for me to speak with [Target Prospect] as we help to solve that issue, and we could likely have a productive conversation.

If the gatekeeper does not know the answer to your question, you can use that as a reason to talk with the target prospect with something like this:

Well, that is why I need to speak with [target prospect] as [he or she] will most likely know the answer to that question.

USE NAME-DROPPING

Another way to disarm gatekeepers is to name-drop other people you have spoken to in the organization so that you don't look like an outsider who is calling to try to work your way in. The way to do that is to say something like this:

I spoke with Tom Jones in accounting, and now I am trying to reach someone in HR. Do you know who the best person for me to connect with is?

By mentioning this, not only will the gatekeeper feel like you must be OK to let in because you are already somewhat on the inside, but he or she will feel like it will not be good to be rude or completely block you out because you appear to already have some existing relationships or business going on with the company.

If you like the logic with this tactic but you feel that you cannot use it because you have not spoken to anyone in the organization yet, you can modify your name-drop to use the names of people you are planning to meet with by saying something like this:

We are planning on meeting with Mary Smith next month, but we need to connect with an operations manager prior to that. Can you help point me in the right direction for who I should reach out to?

You can use this even if you don't have meetings on the schedule because you are saying that you are planning to meet and not that you have a meeting scheduled.

MENTION AN INITIATIVE

You can try to look less like an outsider by mentioning that you are calling to discuss a particular initiative with something like this:

> *I am calling to discuss the initiative to consolidate distribution channels. Can you help me to get connected with the director of operations?*

You can either do some research in news articles and press releases to find initiatives that you can reference. But if you cannot find anything, you can mention a common or generic initiative with something similar to one of these:

- Reduce costs
- Increase sales
- Improve production
- Decrease employee turnover
- Improve customer satisfaction

Try to Befriend the Gatekeeper

It is not a stretch to say that if you can establish a more friendly exchange with the gatekeeper, you can decrease the overall level of resistance that you will face. While this might be easier said than done, here are a couple of things you can do to foster a better relationship:

- **Catch his or her name:** Try to ask for the gatekeeper's name and then use it throughout the conversation. Even though this is very minor, it can help to bring down guardedness.

- **Have a friendly tonality:** The more friendly you sound on the phone, the more friendly a gatekeeper will be. To improve your tonality, if you force yourself to smile when on a call with a gatekeeper, this will change how you sound and can impact how the gatekeeper responds to you.

SHARE THAT YOU UNDERSTAND THEM

There are times where you may feel like you are in a stalemate with a gatekeeper—he or she is not budging on letting you in, and you are not ready to give up. When this happens, you can try to let the gatekeeper know that you understand why he or she is doing this with something like this:

> I understand the situation you are in. You get calls all day from sales-people, and it is your job to not let a bothersome salesperson through. I can tell you that I am not one of those annoying salespeople. I will be very respectful of [Target Prospect]'s time, and there is a very good chance that we can have a very productive conversation because we help [Target Buyer Type] to:
>
> • Value Point 1
> • Value Point 2
> • Value Point 3
>
> What is the best way for me to connect with [Target Prospect]?

AVOIDING THE GATEKEEPER ALTOGETHER

One last tactic that you can do is to find a way to avoid the gatekeeper altogether. A good way to do this is to call when the gatekeeper is not at his or her desk by calling before 8:00 a.m., during the lunch hour, and after 5:00 p.m. If you are calling direct dial phone numbers that are usually routed to a gatekeeper, a target prospect will be more likely to answer his or her own phone during these windows of time.

Gatekeeper Objections

These are the most common objections that gatekeepers will use to try to get rid of you:

- *What is this in regards to?*
- *Is this a sales call?*
- *We are not interested.*
- *We already use someone for that.*
- *We do not need that right now.*
- *Send me your information and I will pass it along.*

Chapter 21 talks about each of those in more detail and provides ideas for how to respond. You can respond to these in a similar way whether you are talking to a gatekeeper or a target prospect. The only difference is if you respond to the objection with a pain question and the gatekeeper gives you an answer that reveals that there might be a pain or concern, you can use that as a reason to talk with the target prospect with something like this:

> *Oh, I see. Well, that is one of the reasons why I am calling because that is exactly the type of thing that we help with. This is why [Target Prospect] would likely find our discussion interesting and a good use of [his or her] time. What is the best way for me to connect with [him or her]?*

Two Types of Gatekeepers

There are two different types of gatekeepers that you will cross paths with when cold calling. They are fairly different and understanding how they differ can help you with knowing how best to deal with them.

FRONT DESK RECEPTIONISTS

Many of the gatekeepers that you will face are front desk receptionists who answer the main phone number. These will probably be the most difficult type of gatekeeper because if they have been given the task of keeping out salespeople, they will try to block out all salespeople without considering whether or not the salesperson should be listened to. In other words, they will be difficult to reason with as to why the prospect should talk to you, and they may try to get rid of you based solely on their impression of you being a salesperson.

This gatekeeper can have a decent amount of knowledge of the organization in terms of who does what and who is best to talk to. But overall, this is a fairly low-level position in the organization, often filled with an employee with less skills or experience. Receptionists will usually be working in hectic work environments where they are multitasking all day by answering the phone, checking in people and deliveries, and servicing employee requests.

EXECUTIVE ASSISTANTS

The second type of gatekeepers is executive assistants, and they usually work for the leaders (executives) of a specific department of the company. For example, the CFO will likely have an executive assistant who will help him or her personally with all sorts of tasks. However, this executive assistant will usually also support other leaders and employees in the finance department from an administrative standpoint. The CFO and other senior leaders in the finance department will often route their phone numbers to the executive assistant, making this person the gatekeeper when you call.

Executive assistants will usually be a little more sophisticated in terms of competence and experience, and this by no means is a low-level position. You might notice this in the way they try to screen you because they may listen to what you have to say and make a more informed decision on how to handle you instead of just trying to get rid of all salespeople. With that, if you can communicate very clearly who you are and why the prospect will want to talk with you, you can increase the odds of this gatekeeper either letting you in, directing you to a better person to contact, or sharing valuable information with you.

Executive assistants will often work closely with the leaders of a department, and this means that they will often have deep knowledge about the department, current issues and priorities, and who does what. Because of this, they can be a great resource for gathering valuable information. If you end up on the phone with an executive assistant and he or she starts to block you out, definitely shift to treating him or her like the target prospect and ask some of your pain and current environment questions. Not only will the executive assistant likely be able to answer many of your questions, but he or she might also appreciate the respect that you are showing by treating him or her like the target prospect.

In some situations, you may end up having an Instant Meeting with an executive assistant where he or she ends up sharing extremely valuable information that you can use for navigating the organization and finding opportunities. In some cases, the executive assistant will provide information that helps you to identify that the organization is not a good fit and that it does not make sense to spend your valuable time trying to get into the account. Or the executive assistant may hear how you help and identify that there is someone else in the organization you should talk with instead of the target prospect. Or after building rapport with the executive assistant, you could try to turn him or her into a coach and ask for help and guidance on communicating with the target prospect.

The key point here is that the executive assistant will appear to be a gatekeeper standing in your way, but if you handle the situation correctly, this person can become a valuable asset that you can leverage during your efforts to try to get into a new account.

Don't Take It Personally

When you get shot down by gatekeepers, it can be easy to let that bother you, and you might take it personally. Sometimes when a gatekeeper says he or she is not interested in your product, it can be easy to feel like that person is rejecting you. Part of that could be because you take pride in your company, and when the gatekeeper rejects your product, it can make you feel rejected personally. Or maybe you take pride in your efforts to be a great salesperson, and when a gatekeeper blocks you out, you can take it personally by feeling that you are not doing a good job.

If any of those feelings occur when you deal with difficult gatekeepers, I want you to try to keep these four things in the front of your mind when you are cold calling:

It has nothing to do with you.

Don't feel bad or take it personally because the gatekeeper's rejection and ugliness has nothing to do with you and who you are as a person.

They are rejecting your company and product.

If anything, the gatekeepers are rejecting your company and product and not you, so don't take it personally. In most situations, gatekeepers are not even rejecting your product as they haven't even fully considered whether or not your product deserves their attention before trying to get rid of you.

They are just doing their job.

The reason that they might be rejecting you before fully considering whether your product deserves the prospect's attention is because their job is to get rid of all salespeople, and this has nothing to do with you, your product, or your company.

Their job is very difficult and unpleasant.

If you get frustrated by a gatekeeper, just remember that the job is difficult and unpleasant. This thought applies more to front desk receptionists as their job is very hectic with the phone ringing, people and deliveries needing to be checked in, employees requesting help, and more. Then, on top of all that, they have salespeople calling all day, where they stand to get in trouble if one happens to sneak by. It can be a difficult, unpleasant, and challenging job that probably does not pay very well. If you can picture some of this when you butt heads with gatekeepers, it might be easier to excuse them for being difficult, and this can help keep you from getting frustrated and letting them ruin your day.

CHAPTER 23

Qualifying the Prospect

There are only so many hours in the day and in the week. There is nothing you can do to get or buy more, and this makes time one of your most valuable resources. You can protect this resource by minimizing the amount of time that you spend with prospects who have a low probability of purchasing from you. The best way to do that is to use a process for qualifying prospects to separate the good from the bad, and we will explain how to do that in this chapter.

Measuring the Quality of the Prospect

In order to qualify a prospect, you have to be able to measure or assess how good or bad the lead is. To get a more accurate assessment, you can measure prospects in four different areas:

1. Need to purchase
2. Ability to purchase
3. Authority to purchase
4. Intent to purchase

For prospects to be completely qualified, they should be strong in all four of these areas. That does not mean that they have to be strong in every area to end up buying from you. More so, we are saying that if a prospect is strong in each of these areas, you can consider that person to be a high-quality prospect, and that can give you more confidence in these areas:

- The prospect has a decent to high probability of purchasing from you.
- This is a prospect that is worth you spending your valuable time with.
- It is fairly safe to forecast revenue for this prospect in your pipeline.
- The prospect should be easy to close at the end of the sales process.

But if you identify that the prospect is weak in any of these four areas, this means that the lead is a lower quality prospect, and you might move forward with these assumptions:

- There is a decent to high probability that something will prevent this prospect from purchasing.
- It might not be wise to spend a lot of your valuable time with this prospect.
- You should be cautious about forecasting this business in your pipeline.
- The prospect could be difficult to close.

Not only will finding out that the prospect is weak in one of the four key areas help you to be more cautious, but identifying which of the four areas that the prospect is weak can provide clues for what you need to do with the prospect, and we will explain that next.

NEED TO PURCHASE

There are times where prospects will seem very interested in what you sell. This is great, but it is important to know if the prospect's interest is tied to more of a "need" or if it is more of a "want." For example, if someone has a car that breaks down periodically, this person has a true need for a new car. But if someone has a car that never breaks down and this person is just bored and wants something new, this is more of a want. It is important to be able to identify which type of interest the prospect has in order to qualify.

How to Handle a No Need Prospect

If you identify that a prospect has more of a want than a need, you should be a little cautious with the amount of time you give them. For example, if you sold cars, you would not want to spend peak hours on a Sunday afternoon taking a prospect on test drives if that person does not really need to purchase a car. You should definitely answer all of his or her questions and provide good customer service, and you can certainly take them on a test drive if there are no other prospects at the dealership. But if there are other prospects that you can spend your valuable time with, you might want to try to find a way to spend more of your time with other prospects who have more of a need for what you sell.

Converting that to a B2B sales scenario, you may have a prospect who asks you to fly across the country to go to her office and give a demo of your product. When she asks for this, you might think that this is qualified lead because she is asking you to come and give a demonstration. But if you were to ask some of your pain, current environment, and qualifying questions, you would find out that, while the prospect is interested in some of the new features of your product, her current system is doing a decent job in most areas. This means that the prospect's interest is more of a want than a need. In this scenario, you definitely want to provide a demonstration and keep the dialogue going, but you might be cautious about spending your time and money to fly out to the prospect's office, and you could do that by proposing a virtual demo.

The other thing you might want to do with a no need prospect is be cautious with how your forecast this business in your pipeline. These are the prospects who are very responsive during the sales process and then go silent or the deal falls apart in the eleventh hour because there is not enough of a need to justify spending the money required to purchase your product.

How to Identify If the Prospect Has a Need

Here are some questions to ask to assess how strong the prospect is in the area of needing what you sell.

Pain Questions

If I could ask you real quick:

- *Pain Question 1*
- *Pain Question 2*
- *Pain Question 3*

Current Environment Questions

- *Who are you currently using today?*
- *How long have you been with them?*
- *How is everything going?*
- *What are some things you like about what they provide?*
- *What are some things that you think could be better?*
- *If you could change one thing about their product/service, what would it be?*
- *When was the last time you considered other options in this area?*
- *(Sizing Question) How many _____ do you currently have?*
- *Are you the right person to discuss this area with?*

Qualifying Questions

Need vs. Want

- *What motivated you to look at us (brought you to us)?*
- *Do you mind if I ask why you took time out of your schedule to meet with us?*
- *What improvements could you see if you make this purchase?*
- *What will happen if you do not purchase something?*
- *Is there a date when this purchase needs to be made?*

- *What happens if the purchase is not made by that date?*
- *What is the time frame that the project needs to work along?*

ABILITY TO PURCHASE

Another area to measure the prospect's qualification is his or her ability to purchase your product in terms of having the needed money or funding. If someone has a car that is periodically breaking down, that person definitely has a need for a new car. But if that person is unemployed and does not have the money needed for the purchase, he or she is weak in the area of having the ability to purchase from a financial standpoint. In the world of B2B sales, this often happens where a prospect completely needs what you sell, but he or she does not have the budget or funding needed to purchase your product.

How to Handle the No Ability Prospect

With this type of prospect, you need to determine if the inability to purchase is temporary or a long-term issue. For example, if a prospect has no funding available today but that could change when the next fiscal year budget opens, the inability to purchase is temporary and could change not too far down the road. This is a helpful detail because it can tell you to be a little cautious but to not completely disqualify the prospect. What that might look like is that you try to stay in touch and invest a medium level of time in the prospect so that you can be there when the ability to purchase improves. But if it is unclear if the prospect will ever have the ability to purchase, you may want to proceed with extreme caution in terms of the amount of time, attention, and priority that you give to the prospect and opportunity.

How to Identify If the Prospect Has the Ability to Purchase

Here are some questions to ask to assess how strong the prospect is in the area of being able to purchase what you sell.

Qualifying Questions

Funding Availability
- *What is the budgetary range that you need this purchase to stay within?*
- *Is there a budget approved for this project?*
- *Have the funds been allocated to this purchase?*
- *What budget (department) will this purchase be made under?*
- *Are there other purchases that this funding may end up being used for?*
- *How does the project fit with other initiatives from a priority standpoint?*

AUTHORITY TO PURCHASE

Authority to purchase means that the prospect has the authority to make the decision to purchase your product. If a prospect has a true need for a new car and has the money needed for the purchase, but it is his or her spouse who makes the final decision on big purchases, then this prospect does not have the authority to purchase. An example of this in B2B sales would be a director of finance who has a true need and budget available for your product, but if it is the VP of finance who will approve the purchase, then the director of finance does not have the authority to purchase your product.

How to Handle the No Authority Prospect

If you learn a prospect does not have decision-making power, you can shift your approach to try to turn the prospect into more of a coach so that this person can help you to identify who the decision maker is. This can often be a delicate situation because your prospect may have an ego and think that he or she is the only person you need to be dealing with. Or the prospect may feel insecure about his or her standing in the organization and not want to bother people higher up with the discussions you are having. In either of those scenarios, the worst thing you could do is ask questions like this:

- *Can you introduce me to [name or title of person with authority to purchase]?*

- *Can you get me a meeting with [name or title of person with authority to purchase]?*

These questions could give the prospect the feeling that you are trying to do something that you should not be doing or that you do not respect him or her and you are trying to get around them. To avoid this, be very direct and say something like this:

Our standard process is to meet with [title of person with authority to purchase] before finalizing the proposal. What is the best way to go about scheduling this?

When you say this in a very direct and confident way, the prospect will have less hesitation and resistance and may help you to get in contact with the person who has decision-making authority. And the goal here is not to change your main point of contact; it is to simply get the person with the authority to purchase to be aware of the discussions you are having so that this person is not completely surprised when you reach the end of the sales process and it is time for the prospect to purchase your product. The optimum scenario would be that the person with authority provides some sort of executive sponsorship or endorsement for the purchase of your product.

If you cannot get that person involved or aware of your discussions, you should begin to seriously question if the prospect is qualified and someone you should spend your valuable time with. If the person who makes the final decision is not available or interested in the discussions that relate to your product, not only could this create issues when it is time to get the purchase approved, but you could also question if there is a true need or if the purchase is important to the organization.

How to Identify If the Prospect Has the Authority to Purchase

Here are some questions to ask that can help to assess how strong the prospect is in the area of having the authority to purchase what you sell.

Qualifying Questions

Decision Authority

- *What is the decision-making process?*
- *What parties will be involved in making the decision?*
- *What are the key factors that a decision will be based on?*
- *What functional areas (departments) will be impacted by the purchase?*
- *Is there a committee that this type of purchase has to go through?*
- *Who is the ultimate decision maker?*
- *Who is the person that will need to sign the agreement/contract?*

INTENT TO PURCHASE

This category measures the prospect's genuine intent to purchase from you. To picture what we are talking about here, imagine a prospect who arrives at a car dealership that needs to purchase a new car, has the money needed for the purchase, and is the ultimate decision maker. Based on strength in those three areas, you could easily view this prospect as being very qualified. But what we do not know is that this prospect has already spent three hours at another dealership where he already performed test drives, decided on a car, and negotiated a price. He then came to the second dealership primarily to get a price comparison to make sure he negotiated a good price at the first dealership. This prospect is weak in the area of genuine intent to purchase from the second dealership because he is very far along in discussions with a competitor and intends to buy from someone else. This type of weakness can be challenging because it is easy to miss, and you can be completely unaware that the prospect has the intent to purchase from someone else.

An example of this in B2B sales is where a prospect sends out an RFP (request for proposal) to many different vendors. When a salesperson receives the RFP, the prospect may appear to be very qualified with all of the details and requirements in the document. That impression would be correct as the prospect most likely has a need to purchase, ability to purchase, and authority to purchase. But the problem is that, in this hypothetical scenario, the prospect is already very far along in discussions with another vendor, and it is actually the other vendor who wrote the RFP and the requirements all match up exactly with the product that the competitor sells. The reason the prospect sent out the RFP was only to comply with a procurement process requirement that requires an RFP to be sent out before certain purchases are made. This means that the prospect does not have the genuine intent to purchase from the other vendors that are sent the RFP.

How to Handle the No Intent Prospect

Identifying that the prospect is very far along in discussions with another vendor does not mean that you cannot persuade him or her to buy from you. More so, it is a reason for you to quickly shift gears in the following areas:

- Be more cautious about the time you spend with the prospect
- Get more aggressive on the price you offer
- Share more information on how you match up against the competition

If we go back to the car example, if you identify that the prospect is extremely far along in discussions with another dealership, this is helpful because you can skip wasting time trying to sell the car. Since you know that the prospect is leaning toward the competition, you can skip all of the negotiating and jump straight to your best price. You can also focus on explaining how you compare and differentiate from the other dealership. You can win this business, but you will need to know what you are dealing with so that you can change your strategy.

For the RFP example, if you receive an unsolicited RFP where it is pretty clear that your competition is already involved, don't spend a week working on the most beautiful proposal because you know it is not a completely qualified prospect. If you want to respond, use boilerplate proposal responses and throw out your best available price and see what happens. In other words, be responsive to requests and questions but don't put a lot of effort, time, and money at risk as there are probably better prospects to focus on.

How to Identify If the Prospect Has the Intent to Purchase

Here are some questions to ask to assess how strong the prospect is in the area of intending to purchase from you.

Qualifying Questions

Level of Competition
- *What other options are you considering?*
- *How far along are you in discussions with them?*
- *How do you feel about your other options?*
- *What do you like about them?*
- *What do you not like about them?*
- *How do they compare with what we have to offer?*
- *Is there a reason why you would choose us over them?*
- *If you had to make a decision today, which way would you lean?*

Two-Step Qualification Process

In Chapter 16, we outlined three sales process steps: Initial Contact, Meeting, and Presentation. In order to align this qualifying process with those sales process steps, we break the qualifying process into two steps: pre-qualifying and qualifying.

STEP 1: PRE-QUALIFYING

The pre-qualifying step is where you try to determine if there is even the slightest fit between what you sell and the prospect's needs in order to determine if it makes sense to have a brief conversation. Your pain and current environment questions will do a good job of identifying what is going on with the prospect and help you to determine if you and the prospect are in the general area of having a reason to keep talking. When you are pre-qualifying the prospect, you don't need to worry about identifying if the prospect has budget available or decision-making power because all you are trying to do is see if it makes sense to start a real conversation. As a result, you do not need to ask any of the qualifying questions at this point.

The only step in the sales process where you want to focus on pre-qualifying is the Initial Contact, and you are pre-qualifying to determine if it makes sense to progress to the Meeting sales process step.

STEP 2: QUALIFYING

The qualifying step is where you try to measure the prospect in the four key areas we just outlined:

1. Need to purchase
2. Ability to purchase
3. Authority to purchase
4. Intent to purchase

As soon as you reach the Meeting sales process step, you should start qualifying the prospect to determine how the prospect measures up in the four key areas and you can use your pain, current environment, and qualifying questions for this.

Qualifying Questions Explained

Here are some more details around why to ask these questions and what to do with the answers.

NEED VS. WANT

What motivated you to look at us? What brought you out today?
If you have an inbound lead that came to your website, store, or business, it can be helpful to know what motivated this person to look at your product. If a car salesperson asks this to a prospect that comes to a dealership and his answer is that his spouse is shopping next door, this tells you that he might not have a true need. But if

his answer is that his current lease is expiring in two months, then he definitely has a need to purchase a car.

Do you mind if I ask why you took time out of your busy schedule to meet with us?

This is a good question to ask when you have a first meeting with a prospect because it can help you to understand what his or her motivation is, and that can tell you if the interest is more of a need or want. For example, if this person took the meeting because an inside sales rep was persistent about getting the appointment on the calendar, the prospect probably doesn't have a need for your product. That is not to say that you cannot have a productive meeting and take it somewhere, but if your prospect answers that he or she took the meeting because the contract with the current provider is expiring at the end of the year and he needs to start considering other options, this question helped you to determine that the prospect has a need for what you sell.

What improvements could you see if you make this purchase?

With all of your product knowledge in your head, you can likely tell the prospect why he or she should buy your product. But getting prospects to tell you in their own words will not only tell you if they need what you sell, but it will also confirm if they understand what your product does and the value that it has to offer.

What will happen if you do not purchase something?

One of your biggest competitors is the status quo: the prospect's option to not do anything. And when trying to identify if the prospect needs what you sell, it can help to understand what the option of not purchasing anything looks like for the prospect. If there is not a major impact to the prospect if he or she decides to hold off on making the purchase, the interest may be more of a want. But if there are problems or inconveniences that start to occur in the scenario where the prospect does not purchase something, then there is more of a need for what you sell.

Is there a date when this purchase needs to be made? What is the time frame that the project needs to work along?

Identifying that the prospect has a deadline means the prospect has more of a need than a want. This question can also uncover valuable information you can use to manage the sales process. For example, if the prospect's current system is being discontinued at the end of the year and he or she needs a replacement by that time, you can then use that piece of information throughout the sales process to keep discussions moving forward.

What happens if the purchase is not made by that date?

If the prospect shares a date when the purchase needs to be made by, that is valuable information. And you can make that information even more valuable by asking what will happen if the prospect is not able to make the purchase by that date. For example, if not having a new system in place when the current system becomes discontinued is a huge problem and will put all current customers' data at risk, this makes the prospect much more qualified in the area of needing to purchase.

FUNDING AVAILABILITY

What is the budgetary range that you need this purchase to stay within?

If you ask a prospect how much he or she has to spend on your product, it can be difficult to get an honest and accurate answer because this is a very invasive question. The prospect might feel uncomfortable sharing that information or be insecure about their financial situation. Or the prospect could see this question as part of your negotiating process and think that the answer he or she gives you will impact the price you quote. With that, the prospect might not answer at all, might answer with a number that is higher than the truth to not lose your respect, or answer with a number that is lower than the truth in order to try to get a better deal from you.

You can avoid all of that by asking prospects what range they are looking to stay within. If you are very direct and a matter of fact when you ask this, you will be surprised how often prospects share the details of what they are able to spend. Allowing prospects to answer with a range also helps as it gives them a little more control over how much information they share when they answer. You can include some example ranges as part of this question which can look like this:

> What is the budgetary range that you need this purchase to stay within? For example, there are projects that can fall in the range of

$1,000 to $10,000, some between $10,000 and $30,000, and some that are between $30,000 and $100,00. Do you know what range your project would fall under?

Is there a budget approved for this project?

This is one way to ask the prospect if he or she has money to spend. If the budget has not been approved, you might want to be a little cautious and work with the prospect to figure out the process and steps needed to get the budget approved.

Have the funds been allocated to this purchase? Are there other purchases that this funding may end up being used for? How does the project fit with other initiatives from a priority standpoint?

If the prospect has budget to spend, that is great. But there are a lot of things that budget dollars can get used for and it can be diligent to ask if the funds have been allocated and set aside for your product. If the funds have not been set aside, you could get surprised at the end of the sales process when another purchase has consumed the budget dollars that you were expecting your prospect to use.

What budget (department) will this purchase be made under?

Many B2B purchases will impact multiple departments. With that, it can be helpful to understand which budget or department is going to fund the purchase of your product.

DECISION AUTHORITY

What is the decision-making process?

While it is important to find out if the prospect is the decision maker, I do not recommend asking "Are you the decision maker?" as I believe that is a flawed question for these reasons:

1. The prospect may have a big ego and want to appear as having decision-making power when he or she does not.

2. The prospect answers that he or she is the decision maker because this person does make some decisions, but the purchase of your product will actually need to be approved by someone higher in the organization and this person is the true decision maker.

3. Your prospect tells you that he or she is the decision maker in order to prevent you from trying to reach out to people higher in the organization.

With all of that being said, a better way to go and actually get more information on the organization is to ask about the process the prospect will have to go through to purchase your product. The optimum answer to this question would be for the prospect to share with you the main steps and key players that would be involved at each step. But in a lot of scenarios, the prospect's answer will either be vague or incomplete, and that is no problem because all you have to do is follow up their answer with this question:

OK, great, And what would need to be done after that?

You will want the explanation to go all the way to the last step of the process where the paperwork is signed or the purchase is processed. Usually when you identify what that step looks like, you will have clarity on who the ultimate decision maker is.

What parties will be involved in making the decision?

While there is usually one ultimate decision maker, there are usually many influencers who will be involved in the process. It might be helpful to become more aware of who is involved so that you can make sure you are communicating with and on the same page with all the key players.

What are the key factors that a decision will be based on?

The prospect may have an organized list of requirements or factors that are being used to measure you and your competitors. This can be extremely helpful to get access to as it can help you to make sure you are communicating clearly in all of the areas that are important to the prospect. If you are very direct in how you ask this question, you will be surprised how often a prospect will tell you the key things you are being measured on.

What functional areas (departments) will be impacted by the purchase?

If you sell a product that impacts multiple departments, there might be stakeholders from the other departments who will play a role in the decision-making process. If you are only talking with one of the departments and do not have any communications or relationships with the other departments that will be impacted by the purchase, your opportunity is not completely qualified and could be seen as weak in the area of authority to purchase.

Is there a committee that this type of purchase has to go through?

It is very important to know if there is a committee that is going to be involved in the decision-making process. This will not only help you with properly managing the opportunity through the prospect's buying process, but it will let you know that the prospect you are dealing with might not have the authority to purchase.

Who is the ultimate decision maker?

You can ask the prospect who the ultimate decision maker is. But as mentioned already, the prospect may just say he or she is when that is not true. My suggestion would be to ask the other decision authority questions and see what information you can get from the prospect. If it is still not clear who the decision maker is, you can just ask the prospect who that person is with this question.

Who is the person that will need to sign the agreement/contract?

Whatever questions you ask the prospect, at some point you may want to ask who signs the paperwork. Even if he or she tells you who the ultimate decision maker is, you can confirm that the person identified is the ultimate decision maker by asking this question. There can be many situations where your prospect tells you one name as the ultimate decision maker, and when you ask this question, the prospect actually ends up providing a different name.

LEVEL OF COMPETITION

What other options are you considering? Who else are you guys looking at?

Don't be afraid to ask the prospect what other vendors he or she is looking at or talking to. In many cases, if you simply ask this question in a very direct way, the prospect will respond and tell you who you are competing against. Being able to find out this information will not only help you to qualify the prospect, it will help you to make sure you have the right strategy in place to try to win the prospect's business.

How far along are you with the other vendors?

If the prospect is talking to other vendors, try to identify how long those discussions have been going on. If the prospect first contacted your competitor around the same time that he or she contacted you, you do not have too much to be concerned about in terms of the prospect's intentions. But if the prospect has been talking to another vendor for three months, you might proceed with caution because you are behind the competition in terms of relationship and discussions, and the prospect may not have genuine intentions to purchase from you.

How do you feel about your other options? What do you like about them? What do you not like about them? How do they compare with what we have to offer?

There is nothing wrong with directly asking the prospect how he or she feels about your competition. You can likely tell the prospect all of the ways you are better than the competition, but it is more powerful to get the prospect to share how he or she feels. Not only will this tell you if the prospect's knowledge of how you compare to the competition is correct, but the answer will also give you a good idea about which way he or she is leaning.

Is there a reason why you would choose us over them?

Salespeople often spend most of their time telling prospects why they should buy the salesperson's product. But when you are talking with a prospect about the different options being considered, it can be extremely powerful to ask the prospect if there are any reasons why he or she would choose you over the competition.

247

Just to explain the delivery of this question, it is delivered not from an insecure standpoint where you are doubting why the prospect should buy from you. More so it is delivered with confidence, and you are giving an opportunity for the prospect to answer this in his or her own words. You will be ready to tell the prospect why he or she should buy from you, and you can educate them if needed. But if the prospect can answer this question without your help, this will be a very positive indicator that this person is favorable to your product and understands the value that your product has to offer.

If you had to make a decision today, which way would you lean?

This can be a good litmus test question to try to figure out where you stand against your competition. If the prospect is leaning toward your competitor, this can either tell you that you need to change your strategy in order to win the business, or it can tell you to be more cautious about the time you spend on the prospect moving forward.

CHAPTER 24

Closing

Many salespeople view closing as the key thing they need to improve in order to sell more. I personally believe that if you do the right things during the sales process, closing should be the easiest step. And in some cases, deals will almost close themselves. I will explain how that works in this chapter.

Indirect Closing Techniques

Everything that we have discussed up to this point in this book will indirectly make closing sales prospects much easier.

A Good Sales Message Makes Closing Easier

If you use the SMART Sales System process to create a consultative selling sales message, you should find it easier to close prospects because you will likely:

- Clearly communicate what you do, how you help, and what problems you can solve
- Be more effective at making the prospect interested in what you sell
- Trigger less guardedness
- Build more rapport and better relationships by not being a pushy salesperson
- Establish more trust and credibility

Qualifying the Prospect Makes Closing Easier

One of the reasons closing can be difficult is that we often end up trying to close prospects who do not need or cannot buy what we sell. With that, if you do a better job at filtering out bad prospects, you will end up trying to sell to prospects that fit better in terms of needing and being able to purchase what you sell, and this will make closing easier. Using a thorough process for qualifying will help to separate good prospects from bad, immediately making you a better closer.

Being Prepared for Objections Makes Closing Easier

When you are not able to close a prospect, you are likely being stopped by some sort of objection. By being more prepared for objections, you will improve your ability to handle these situations and keep conversations going. This will help you to stay engaged longer, giving you multiple opportunities to close, which should have a positive impact on your close rate overall.

Direct Closing Techniques

While there are many things you can do to indirectly make closing easier, there are also some more direct things that you can do to improve how you close prospects and those are discussed in this section.

TRIAL CLOSING

Trial closing is performing a "test" close to identify where the prospect is in terms of his or her level of interest. Here are some examples of what that might look like:

- *What do you think about what you have seen so far?*
- *How do you think this fits with what you are needing?*
- *How would that feature help you?*
- *Is this something you could see your organization using?*
- *Are we heading in the right direction?*
- *Is this what you were expecting to see?*

These questions will help you get a better understanding of what the prospect is thinking, and this will help you to know if you are heading in the right direction or if you need to make any adjustments. With that, you don't have to wait until it is time to close to ask your trial closing questions; you can ask some of these every time you speak with the prospect and that will help you to communicate better throughout the sales process, which will ultimately make closing prospects easier.

ASSUMPTIVE CLOSE

An assumptive close is just assuming the prospect is wanting to move forward when you try to close. For example, if you are trying to schedule a prospect for a free consultation, an assumptive close for this might look like the following:

> We do free consultations every day at 10:00 a.m. What day works best for you?

This basically skips asking if the prospect wants to move forward and jumps to the next question that would be asked.

ALTERNATIVE CLOSE

The alternative close is a different variation of the assumptive close where you give the prospect two options with the assumptive close. Staying with the same example:

> We do our free consultations on Tuesdays and Thursdays. Which day works best for you?

TURN QUESTIONS INTO STATEMENTS

One minor tactic to help you with closing is to turn questions into statements. To demonstrate with an example that is not related to selling, let's say you are trying to get someone to agree to eat at a particular restaurant. Here is how you might ask the other person to do that:

Do you want to go eat at Max's Grill?

If you simply change that from a question to a statement, you might end up saying something like this:

Let's go eat at Max's Grill.

The difference between the two is very subtle, but that small change could decrease how much time the other person spends thinking about what he or she wants to eat. And by you decreasing the time the other person spends thinking, you might decrease the odds that the other person disagrees with what you are suggesting.

Here is how that might apply to a selling situation:

- **Question:** *Do you want to meet next week to see a demonstration?*

- **Statement:** *Let's meet next week and I will show you a demonstration.*

LET THE PROSPECT LEAD (SOFT CLOSE)

One of the most powerful ways to close a prospect is to simply ask what he or she wants to do next. Here are some examples of what that might look like:

- *What would you like to do next?*
- *What direction do you want to go from here?*
- *Do you want to continue talking about this?*
- *When would you like to talk again?*
- *What does the path forward look like?*

When you close in this way, you can have more confidence in the prospect's level of interest compared to a prospect you have to pressure into moving forward. Closing in this way can also help to build rapport with the prospect because you are being less pushy and more respectful. This increased rapport can improve information sharing, responsiveness, and the overall relationship, all of which will greatly improve your ability to close the sale at the end of the process.

HARD CLOSING QUESTIONS

Whether you use a soft closing style or not, there are certainly times when you need to ask questions that are a little more firm, and here are some examples of hard closing questions:

- *Are you ready to move forward to the next step in the process?*
- *What would you need to be able to make a commitment to move forward?*
- *If you had everything that you are asking for, are you prepared to move forward?*
- *When are you going to make your final decision?*
- *(If delaying the decision for a period of time) OK, but do you mind if I ask if there will be a change or something different at that time that will make it a better time to look at moving forward?*
- *Is there anything that is preventing you from being able to move forward with this purchase?*

PARTNERSHIP PLAN

One tool that you can use to improve your closing process is a partnership plan. This is basically a document that lists out all of the steps that you and the prospect will take together leading up to the purchase and implementation of your product. Here is an example:

Activity	Due Date	Owner	Status
Initial Meeting	11/05/2019	Michael Jones Dennis Martin	Complete
Presentation / Demonstration	11/16/2019	Michael Jones Dennis Martin Veronica Flores	Complete
Discovery Meeting	11/23/2019	Michael Jones Stan Wilson	Open
X Corp to provide requirements	11/29/2019	Stan Wilson	Open
Presentation of draft proposal and contract language	12/2/2019	Michael Jones	Open
Communication of change requests to documents	12/5/2019	Dennis Martin	Open
Delivery of final executable documents	12/12/2019	Michael Jones	Open
Partnership agreement signed	12/19/2019	Tech Bee / X Corp	Open
Implementation begins	1/15/2020	Tech Bee / X Corp	Open
Go live	4/1/2020	X Corp	Open

This sales tool is just a table with rows for the main tasks that need to be completed with details for the due date, people involved, and the status for each task. To create a partnership plan, fill in this table with all of the details that you can think of and then either put this at the end of your presentation slide deck or at the end of your proposal. A good time to share this is at the end of your Presentation sales step by saying something like this:

> If you would like to keep moving forward, this is what our partnership plan looks like. These are some of the steps that need to be taken between now and you getting up and running.
>
> Based on what we discussed today, are you interested in moving forward with this plan?

If the prospect is hesitant to commit to the plan, you can decrease what you are asking for by only trying to get commitment on the next step in the plan with something like this:

> *OK, no problem at all. Do you have enough interest to move to the*
> *next step on this partnership plan?*

Whether you are able to get commitment to the full plan or just the next step, you need to work with the prospect to finalize the partnership plan by making any needed additions or changes to the list of steps. You can try to get the prospect to participate in that by asking this:

> *Great. Do these steps and time estimates look correct and acceptable*
> *to you?*

> *Do you have anything that you want to add or change?*

From there, work with the prospect to make any adjustments or additions in terms of adding or removing any steps, changing any dates, adding or changing any of the owners of certain tasks, etc.

This closing tool will serve two purposes for you. First, it is a great tool to use at the end of the Presentation sales step to close the prospect on committing to move forward and get his or her agreement on all of the required steps. The second thing this tool will help with is keeping the prospect accountable through all of the different steps that you need to go through. For example, if the prospect tries to delay a meeting until next month, you can point back to the partnership plan and say something like:

> *Sure, we can definitely delay the meeting. But according to our agreed*
> *upon partnership plan, you want to have the system implemented by*
> *January 1st, and if we delay the meeting to next month, that will likely*
> *impact your ability to be up and running by January 1st.*

Do we need to change the target date of January 1st or do you want to try to meet earlier than next month so that you can still hit your go live date?

COMPELLING EVENT

A compelling event is a date of significance for the prospect regarding his or her need to purchase your product. For example, if the prospect is looking at replacing a current vendor and the current contract expires on December 31st, that date is a compelling event as the prospect likely needs to have the new vendor in place by December 31st.

When you know a prospect has a compelling event, this can help with closing because you can use the date to keep the prospect moving forward by creating a sense of urgency. For example, if a prospect is not replying to your emails, you could say something like this in your next email and voicemail message:

I noticed that I never heard back from you on my last two messages. No problem at all. I know you all are busy with your [project]. But you mentioned needing a replacement for your current vendor by December 31st.

If you want to continue exploring us as one of your replacement options, we will need to complete our [specific sales process step] by October 31st in order to keep everything on track to make sure you are switched over by your target date. With that, please let me know when you can jump on a quick call to discuss what direction makes the most sense from here.

Some good areas to look for compelling events are contracts expiring, current systems being discontinued, sites being opened or moved, changes in the company or organization, budgets expiring, etc. The best way to learn of compelling events is to ask questions that help you to learn what is going on with the prospect and many of the current environment and qualifying questions will help with that.

However, you may find yourself in a situation where there is absolutely no date of significance for the prospect in terms of when he or she needs to purchase your product. In this case, you can manufacture a compelling event by offering a discount or promotion that expires on a particular day. The expiration date for the discount will become a compelling event that you can use to create a sense of urgency to motivate the prospect to continue to move forward through the sales process.

SALES TAKEAWAY

One of the more powerful closing tactics is the sales takeaway. This tactic is where the salesperson switches from trying to get the prospect to buy the product to trying to take away the option for the prospect to buy the product.

How to Do a Sales Takeaway
Here are three ways to take away the product that you are selling.

Express Doubt
Express doubt that the prospect needs what you sell or is the right person to talk with. Here are some examples:

- *I do not know if you need what we provide.*
- *I do not know if you are a good fit with what we do.*
- *I do not know if we can help you in the same way that we have helped others.*
- *I do not know if you are interested in those improvements.*
- *I do not know if you are concerned about those areas.*
- *I do not know if you are the right person to speak with.*
- *I do not know if it makes sense for us to talk.*
- *Maybe this is not the right time for you to look at this purchase.*
- *Maybe we are not the right product for you.*
- *Maybe this is more than you need right now.*

When in Doubt, Call It Out

If you start seeing some warning signs that the prospect does not need what you sell or is not very interested, you could perform a sales takeaway by calling out what you are concerned about and playing it back to the prospect. For example, if a prospect does not appear to have any pain or challenges, you could reply with something like this:

> *Well, it sounds like you guys have done a good job of putting all of the right pieces in place. Maybe it does not make sense for us to spend too much time talking.*

Or if the prospect has a pretty good system in place, you could perform a takeaway by sharing your concern with something like this:

> *Well, I am a little concerned. You seem very interested in our system, and that is great. But your current system is working pretty well. I am worried that our teams may spend a lot of valuable time, and then you might have trouble getting funding for this because the current system is working pretty well.*

Sarcasm

If you are getting mixed signals from the prospect in terms of interest, you could perform a sales takeaway by using sarcasm. For example, if you are meeting with a prospect and he or she appears to have zero interest in what you are saying and appears to not even want to be there, you could do a sales takeaway with sarcasm to see what is going on by saying something like:

> *Well, you seem excited to be meeting with us today.*

The tonality you use here is critical as you don't want to sound rude or attacking. The key here is to say this in a way where you are trying to be humorous, and if you do not know how to do that, you may want to refrain from doing a sales takeaway by using sarcasm.

When to Do a Sales Takeaway

You may read those sales takeaway examples and wonder why a salesperson would ever say anything like that to a prospect. The key thing here is when to do the takeaway as there are certain moments where this can be a good thing to do. One simple way to look at this is that you may want to do a sales takeaway when your prospect is "on the fence" and between the positions of interested in moving forward and not interested at all. To help picture that, here are three potential positions that your prospect could be in:

> **Position #1—Positive (Interested):** This is where the prospect is displaying a high level of interest in your product.

> **Position #2—Neutral (On the Fence):** This where the prospect could be described as indifferent or undecided regarding where he or she stands on purchasing your product.

> **Position #3—Negative (Not Interested):** This is a prospect who is clearly communicating no interest in purchasing what you sell either in what he or she says or by not responding at all.

When you can lay out those three situations, it is easy to see that it only makes sense to perform a takeaway when a prospect is on the fence as you might be able to trigger some movement in one direction or another. For prospects who are interested, you would never want to do a takeaway because the prospect appears to be moving forward. For prospects who are not interested, there is no reason to do a takeaway because the prospect has already performed his or her own takeaway.

What Happens When You Do a Takeaway

Here are the three potential reactions you can anticipate when you do a sales takeaway.

> **Potential Reaction #1—No reaction:** There is the possibility that the prospect has no real reaction to your sales takeaway, which is not likely because the sales takeaway is a fairly bold thing to do.

But when considering all possible outcomes, no reaction should be included.

Potential Reaction #2—The prospect confirms the takeaway:
The prospect could confirm the doubt you express. For example, if a prospect keeps rescheduling your meetings, you might try to do a sales takeaway with the following:

Sure, we can reschedule. But maybe this is just not the right time for you to look at this right now.

After that takeaway, a prospect could confirm the doubt by saying something like this:

You know, it is really not. Tell you what, let's try to meet after the new year. I will just be wasting your time with any meeting attempts prior to that.

Using a sales takeaway that a prospect accepts or confirms may seem like a bad situation where you shouldn't have done a takeaway. But as long as you are using this tactic at the right time, this outcome will actually be a good thing as it will decrease the time you waste on prospects who are most likely not going to purchase from you.

In this example, if you did not do the takeaway, you would have wasted time rescheduling more meetings or meeting with someone who is not fully present and too busy to look at what you have to offer. This can be a good thing if you repurpose the time saved by looking for more qualified prospects who are interested and available to look at what you have to offer.

Potential Reaction #3—The prospect challenges the takeaway:
The prospect could challenge the doubt that you expressed. Staying

with the same example, the prospect could challenge your doubt with something like:

No, no, no...I am sorry for all of the rescheduling. This is important. I have just been getting hit in all different directions. I do need to look at this right now as we need to figure out what we are going to do before the end of the year. I will block out my entire morning on the 8th for this. Does that work for you?

As you can see in this example, the takeaway triggers a response and more action from the prospect by getting him or her to challenge the doubt that you expressed. If the prospect is strong in the qualification areas of need to purchase, ability to purchase, authority to purchase, and intent to purchase, there is a very good chance that the prospect will challenge your sales takeaway, and this will trigger movement in a positive direction.

When the prospect challenges your takeaway, pay close attention because he or she will often share new information when explaining why it makes sense to keep moving forward. In the example above, this prospect explains how he needs to figure out what he is going to do before the end of the year. If this is new information for the salesperson, this is an example of how the takeaway helped the salesperson to identify new information and a compelling event that he or she was unaware of before performing the takeaway.

Why Use the Sales Takeaway

The interesting thing about this sales tactic is that you could not use a more counterintuitive approach. You are a salesperson who needs to close deals, and you are going to tell a prospect that he or she might not be a good fit? And this is going to help you to increase sales? Yes. This is a result of six powerful things that can occur when using the sales takeaway tactic.

1. Increase rapport: With the sales takeaway, you are doing the exact opposite of what most salespeople do as they will usually push the prospect to move forward 100 percent of the time. And when the prospect is on the fence, the average salesperson will likely increase his or her level of aggressiveness and try harder. By not doing that and actually taking away the product that you sell, you will not only stand out from the majority of other salespeople, but you will display qualities such as confidence, integrity, humility, intelligence, directness, etc. When a prospect sees these characteristics all at once, you are likely to see a significant spike in the level of rapport you have with the prospect.

2. Increase credibility: Similar to the spike in rapport, you can increase the amount of credibility you have with the prospect. This is because when you express doubt, you are showing that you care about what is best for the prospect instead of what is best for you, displaying that you have integrity. If you have integrity and appear to be honest, the prospect will trust you more.

3. Improve the quality of leads in your pipeline: When you perform a sales takeaway, some of your prospects will confirm your doubt, leading to you ending those discussions or putting them on hold. This will help clear out some of the bad leads and opportunities in your pipeline, which can improve your ability to forecast more accurately and free up time to find better prospects.

4. Get stalled deals to move forward: When you get a prospect to challenge your sales takeaway, this will often get stalled deals and on the fence prospects to move forward.

5. Learn new information: When a prospect challenges your sales takeaway, the prospect may share new information as part of an explanation to keep moving forward. Be sure to listen closely to what he or she says as this could be valuable information that you might not have learned if you did not perform a sales takeaway.

6. Improve your close rate: All of these improvements should lead to an improvement in your ability to close prospects. If you are positively impacting any of the areas of rapport, credibility, quality of pipeline, deal momentum, and uncovering new information, it is very safe to assume that you could see an overall improvement in your ability to close.

CHAPTER 25

Networking

Professional networking can be one of the most effective and productive methods for generating leads. In this chapter, I will discuss key things that can turn you into an awesome networker.

Core Concepts

Just about all of the core concepts discussed at the beginning of the book are important for being a good networker, and here is how they come into play.

UNDERSTAND THE PROSPECT

Being a good networker is all about building good relationships. And one of the best ways to build better relationships is to focus more on trying to understand the people you meet and talk to. Not only will this help you to gather valuable information that you can use find opportunities, but it will also make you a more pleasant and enjoyable person for others to talk to.

PROSPECTS GET SOLD TO A LOT

The people that you meet while networking will get sold to a lot. Not only will they probably receive a lot of calls and emails from salespeople, but they will also get sold to a lot at networking events.

DON'T SOUND LIKE A SALESPERSON

Because the people you meet get sold to a lot, you will make a much better impression if you can avoid looking like a salesperson who is trying to sell something when networking.

FOCUS ON OTHERS' INTERESTS, NOT YOURS

If you simply try to focus conversations on the other person's interests instead of yours, you can become a much more interesting and enjoyable person to talk to. This will also help you to build more rapport with the people that you meet, improving your ability to create new relationships.

THE BEST SALESPERSON ASKS THE BEST QUESTIONS

The best way to get the conversation focused on the other person's interests is to simply ask good questions. For example, if you simply start a conversation by asking questions about what the other person does and his or her business, the focus and attention will be more on the other person than on you.

PROSPECTS ARE LIKELY NOT IN BUYING MODE

It is good to assume that the people you meet while networking are not in buying mode for what you sell. This does not mean that they do not need what you sell or can't be sold to. More so, it is most likely the case that they are not thinking about buying what you sell when you meet and talk to them at a networking event.

DON'T SELL THE PRODUCT, SELL THE MEETING

Since the people you meet get sold to a lot and are likely not in buying mode, avoid trying to sell your product when networking. Instead, focus on selling one-on-one conversations with people that you meet when there appears to be a good reason to talk more.

Mindset Changes

The first thing to do in order to be a better networker is to improve your mindset, and this will involve adjustments if three different ways.

SHIFT FROM PICKING FRUIT TO PLANTING SEEDS

Let's stop to think about what farmers do. They will plant seeds, nurture those seeds with light and water, and then at some point down the road, they will pick fruit that grew from the seeds. When farmers are planting the seeds, they will plant many more seeds than they expect to grow, and they will not spend time looking at each seed wondering if it is a seed that will produce fruit. Instead, they nurture all the seeds and focus more on the process. When it is time to pick the fruit, the farmer will have a different mindset and look very closely at each piece of fruit to determine if it is ready to be picked.

This is helpful to keep in mind because it is easy to have the fruit picking mindset when networking by looking closely at each person to determine if he or she is someone who is likely to buy from you. This is very understandable because a salesperson might either have a quota to hit or simply want to make more commissions and money. But this not a good mindset because the people you meet are probably not in buying mode for what you sell, and you also have to talk to a lot of different people before meeting someone where there is a potential fit of some sort. If you are in fruit picking mode, you might think too much and be too critical about the people you talk with and the events you attend. This would be the equivalent of the farmer looking closely at each seed wondering if it is going to produce fruit.

A better way to go is to have the planting seeds mindset by going to many different events and talking with as many people as you can without worrying about who is going to buy from you. Try to nurture the people you meet with attention and inquisitive questions, and see which contacts and conversations grow into something more. When conversations are productive, those contacts will advance forward in your sales process, and it is at that point where you can start to have more of a fruit picking mindset by looking at each contact closely to determine how much time you should invest in the relationship and conversation. Asking your qualifying questions is the equivalent of the farmer being in fruit picking mode and looking closely at each piece of fruit to determine if it is ready to be picked.

LOOK FOR PARTNERS, NOT PROSPECTS

The people that you meet at networking events can likely be put into three categories:

1. **Potential prospects:** These are people who could potentially buy from you at some point.

2. **Networking partners:** These are people who will probably never purchase from you, but they could be individuals you can exchange value with in terms of information, introductions, referrals, etc.

3. **No fit at all:** These are people who will likely never buy from you and don't fit with you at all in terms of being able to collaborate in any way.

With quotas to hit and commissions to make, it can be understandable for salespeople to go to networking events and look for potential prospects. But to become a better networker, try to shift to primarily looking for networking partners. This is simply a shift in what you are thinking about when you first talk with someone. For example, if you meet someone and have the mindset of looking for networking partners, you are more focused on learning about the other person and exploring if there is some sort of opportunity to exchange value in terms of sharing tips, introductions, referrals, etc. Sure, your conversation may lead to identifying the other person as a potential prospect, but the first thing you are thinking about is networking with him or her.

This mindset shift can change how you talk to someone at a networking event as it will help you to be less about you and more about the other person. Not only will this help you to make a better impression, but it is also actually more advantageous to find networking partners than prospects. A good networking partner can lead to multiple introductions, referrals, and new customers, where as a prospect can only lead to one customer in most cases. And in situations where you end up identifying that someone you meet while networking is a great prospect for you, he or she might be more open to hearing about what you sell if you first started the conversation by treating him or her as a potential networking partner.

THE RULE OF RECIPROCITY

As you build relationships with people you meet at networking events, try to use a mindset of reciprocity. Reciprocity is a social rule that is based on the logic that people should repay, in kind, what another person has provided. With that logic, if you try to help your networking partners with introductions and referrals, many of them should be motivated to repay you by bringing introductions and referrals to you.

One way to incorporate this while networking is to try to think about introductions you can make when someone is telling you about what he or she does. If you can think of a helpful introduction, either share the info at the event or in a follow-up email after the event. This small gesture can be a very big deposit in the reciprocity bank account you have with the other person. Regardless of where the introduction goes, just the simple fact that you showed interest in trying to help him or her will foster a positive relationship and could motivate that person to repay you by sharing introductions and referrals with you. And just think what that person will think of you if your introduction has a big impact on his or her life; this person will never forget you.

Getting Out There

It can be extremely easy to find reasons (excuses) to not go to networking events. Not only can we be reluctant because events are often in the evening and after long work days, but there can also be a level of social anxiety that can be felt when thinking about going to something that will involve talking to strangers. To minimize the excuses and reluctance, try to set a quota for yourself for the number of events you need to go to. The number that you set as a goal can vary depending on your situation, but some examples of networking goals could be one networking event per week, per day, or per month.

Whatever goal you set, there are usually enough events in any major city to accommodate your needs. But the first thing you need to do is set a clear goal for yourself and lock it in with an unwavering determination to hit your target without letting any excuses get in your way. When you find events that you are interested in going to, put them on your calendar and treat them like appointments with prospects in the same way that you would only cancel under extreme circumstances.

Finding Events

The first step you can take to get yourself out there networking is to research available events and here are some places you may want to look.

INDUSTRY ASSOCIATIONS

Industry associations will usually have many different events, and there are likely a few industries that you could probably look into.

- The industry for the product that you sell
- The industry for your target buyer
- The industry for your educational background
- The industry for any skills that you have
- The industry for any interests or hobbies that you have

LOCAL NEWS RESOURCES

Check out local newspapers and news websites as they often publish and promote events, groups, and associations in the local area.

SOCIAL MEDIA AND EVENT SITES

Social media platforms are great places for you to find networking events and networking groups. You can also go to different event sites and search engines and search for keywords related to your business or interests to find events.

ALUMNI ASSOCIATIONS

Alumni associations are great places to look for networking events. If you went to a particular school, do some online searches to see if there are any events or activities in your area.

LOCAL UNIVERSITIES

You can also skip the alumni route and just go directly to the websites for universities that are in your area and check out their events calendar. There are often speakers and a variety of different types of events on college campuses that are wide open to anyone who wants to go.

CHARITABLE AND VOLUNTEER ORGANIZATIONS

Getting involved in local charities or volunteer organizations is a great way to expand your network and meet very interesting and high caliber people in your local area. You may think that you would not find any prospects at this type of events. That could be true, but keep in mind that you are not looking for prospects—your goal is to grow your collection of networking partners, and you never know who you will meet at an event. If you can establish someone as a networking partner, you could have access to that person's network of contacts, and that is where there could be target prospects for what you sell.

Networking Sales Process

In the same way that you take prospects through a structured set of sales process steps, you should also take networking partners through a sales process, and you can use the exact same steps with a few minor differences.

INITIAL CONTACT

In most outbound sales situations, your Initial Contact sales process step is a phone call or an email. When networking, your Initial Contact is usually meeting someone at a networking event. And just like how I recommend that your keep your cold calls to two to five minutes, you should also keep your Initial Contact conversations at networking events fairly short, trying to keep them to five to ten minutes. The reason that I suggest keeping it short is that you should try to meet as many people as possible and keeping your conversations short will help you to increase the number of people you are able to meet.

There will certainly be situations where you end up having long conversations with people you meet while networking. The problem with this is that you are likely progressing to the Meeting sales step in the form of an Instant Meeting. And just like how there are reasons to avoid Instant Meetings when cold calling, it is also important to avoid them when networking because the time at an event is very brief and valuable. If you get locked into a long conversation, you are a sacrificing all of the other conversations and people that you could have met during that one conversation, decreasing the number of people you can meet. If you end up in a good conversation and you have been talking for a while, you can say something like this to not only move on to meet someone new, but to also close the contact on moving to the next step in the sales process:

You know, we are actually getting into a good conversation here, and I want to talk more about this. What do you think about pausing right here and getting back together on another day over coffee to talk more? That way I can learn more about what you are doing.

MEETING

The Meeting sales process step for networking partners should be very similar to what you do with prospects. You can meet with them and try to spend the first half of the meeting trying to learn about them, and then spend the second half of the meeting talking about you. When they are sharing what they do with you, try to think about ways that you can help them. This will help you to make a deposit in the reciprocity bank account, which could motivate the other person to try to help you.

In some cases, the Meeting is enough time to learn about each other and it does not make sense to move forward to the Presentation sales step. When this is the case, the close at the end of the Meeting could be a discussion around agreeing to work together and figuring out the best way to stay in touch and share leads. However, in some cases, it does make sense to move forward to the Presentation step and this is when you need to show more information on what you do and sell. This will not only make the partner more able to find referrals for you, but they will also be more likely to keep you in mind. When you advance to the Presentation step with networking partners, the best way to do this would be to go through the Presentation step twice: once for you to present what you do and then again for the networking partner to present what he or she does. One way to propose this is by saying something like this:

There is a lot for us to talk about here. Why don't we break this down and schedule a meeting where we only talk about your stuff and you can explain or show me what you do. After that, we can get back together on another day where I can show you more information on what I do. That way, we will both have a better understanding of each other and will be better able to work together and find referrals for one another.

PRESENTATION

If you progress to the Presentation sales process step, it can look very similar to what you would do for a prospect. In fact, that is probably the best way to educate your networking partner is to treat that person like a prospect by delivering the same presentation and sales pitch. If you normally deliver an online demonstration to your prospects, go through a similar process for with your networking partners. If you flip through a brochure of options while sitting next to your prospects, do something similar when explaining what you do.

Using Your Sales Message While Networking

Here is how to use your consultative selling sales message while networking.

EXPLAINING WHAT YOU DO

One of the most common questions that you will get asked when networking is "What do you do?" How you answer this question will not make or break you, but you can make one small change in how you answer that question to greatly improve the impression you make. Here is how some salespeople answer the "What do you do?" question:

- *I sell [Product].*
- *I work for [Company].*
- *I am a [Product Category] salesperson.*
- *I am in [Product Category] sales.*

Not only do all of those responses break the rule of don't sound like a salesperson, but they are also very boring answers that create minimal opportunity for deeper dialogue. To prevent all of that, answer this question with your value points with a response like this:

Value Points

I help [Target Buyer Type] to:

- *Value Point 1*
- *Value Point 2*
- *Value Point 3*

This is a more intriguing answer that can create curiosity for a continued discussion about what you do, and it will give an impression that you are a little more sophisticated than the other people who are answering with the standard salesperson response.

You may be thinking that saying this does not really answer what the other person is looking for when asking what you do. With that being the case, after you share your value points, one of two things will happen: either the person you are talking to will stare at you, waiting for you to expand on what you just said, or he or she will ask how you do that. In either of those situations, you can continue to explain what you do by sharing some of your product building block.

Product

And I do that by providing [Product] which includes:

- *Feature 1*
- *Feature 2*
- *Feature 3*

Differentiation

Some ways that we differ from other options out there are:

- *Differentiation 1*
- *Differentiation 2*
- *Differentiation 3*

Impact of Doing Nothing

Some things to be concerned with when not doing anything in this area are:

- *Pain Point 1*
- *Pain Point 2*
- *Pain Point 3*

Company Bragging Points

Other key details about us are:

- *Company Fact 1*
- *Company Fact 2*
- *Company Fact 3*

At the end of that, not only will the other person have more information and a better understanding about what you do, but it will likely be a more engaging exchange.

Sometimes when you explain what you do and get into the features of your product, you can begin to lose someone in terms of his or her ability to understand what you are talking about. If this happens, you can use your pain points to try to wrap up the explanation and simplify what you are explaining by saying something like this:

Pain Points

Basically, we work with [Target Buyer Type] and help them solve the challenges of:

- *Pain Point 1*
- *Pain Point 2*
- *Pain Point 3*

ASKING GOOD QUESTIONS

Here are some networking questions that are designed to help you to learn more about a potential networking partner:

Networking Questions

- *How is your day going so far?*
- *What do you do?*
- *How long have you been doing that?*
- *What did you do before?*
- *What do you like most about what you do?*
- *Is there something that motivated you to get into that type of work?*
- *Where are you from?*
- *What brought you to this event?*
- *Have you found this to be a productive event for you?*
- *Are there any other networking events that you recommend?*
- *How can I help you to be successful?*
- *What does a good prospect look like for you?*
- *What is the best way to stay in touch?*
- *What is the best way to work together?*

You can also ask your current environment questions to potential networking partners. Even though these questions are designed for talking with prospects, they are effective at helping you to learn more about what is going on with networking partners.

Getting into Conversations

The key to getting the best ROI for the time, effort, and money that you spend networking is to meet as many people as you can at each event that you go to. That can sometimes be easier said than done because it can sometimes seem difficult to talk to people and break into conversations. With that being the case, here are some tips to get the absolute most out of the time that you have to work with.

GO TO EVENTS ALONE WHEN POSSIBLE

After finding a networking event to go to, your next thought might be to figure out who you can get to go with you. I would not worry too much about this because you will get much more out of a networking event if you go alone. If you go with people you know, you will spend a large portion of the time at the event talking to them and this will decrease the number of people that you meet. If you are on your own, you will replace time spent talking to people you already know with conversations with new contacts. You will also have more people start conversations with you if you do not appear to be talking with a friend or colleague.

ARRIVE WHEN THE EVENT STARTS

When people go to events of any kind, they usually do not want to be the first to arrive as there is a belief that this shows some type of social weakness. This is why many people will try to show up fashionably late by arriving thirty to forty-five minutes after the event start time.

When you are networking, try to completely avoid this way of thinking and try to arrive as close to the event start time as you can. If you do this, you may indeed end up being the first attendee to arrive, and that is completely OK because you will benefit tremendously from the following:

> **Meet the hosts:** If you are one of the first attendees to arrive, you may have the opportunity to meet the people who are hosting and working the event. Not only could some of these people be great

connections to make, but meeting and getting to know the people in charge will raise your level of social status at that particular event.

Become a host: If you are one of the first attendees to arrive, you can almost take an informal host role by greeting and meeting people as they arrive. While you might think you will look weak walking into an event as one of the first attendees, when others arrive after you and see you already established, you will actually appear to be stronger in terms of social status.

Easier to meet people: If you arrive to an event thirty to sixty minutes after it has started, a lot of attendees will have already arrived and everybody will be talking with someone. When you walk into this type of environment, it can be a little chaotic trying to figure out who to talk to and how to break into conversations. But if you arrive when the event starts, there will be less attendees, and many of them will not be talking to anyone. This is a much easier environment to work with in terms of starting conversations with people that you do not know. And when the attendees first arrive and don't know anyone yet, they will be more welcoming to your attempt to start a conversation.

Get the most out of the event: A networking event is a concentration of people that you do not know in a room for a fixed amount of time. You goal should be to meet as many of these people as you can. If you arrive late on purpose, you are decreasing the amount of time you have to work with, and that will lead to a lower ROI for your effort, money, and time. Get the most out of the event by arriving when it starts and staying as long as you can.

TALK TO PEOPLE WHO ARE ALONE

You will often see people at the event standing off to the side not talking to anyone. These are good people for you to warm up with because in most cases they will be very friendly and happy that you are saving them from the discomfort of standing alone.

POST UP IN HIGH TRAFFIC AREAS

Another way to get into conversations is to stand or spend time in high traffic areas. An example of this would be getting a coffee from a refreshment area and then standing near that area as you drink your coffee. When other attendees go to that same area to get a coffee, you can say hello and introduce yourself as they walk by.

JOIN A TABLE OF STRANGERS

Some events will have tables where people sit down to eat, either informally at any time or with a formal meal. In either case, it is completely acceptable for you to sit and eat at a table with people who are complete strangers. Shortly after you sit down at the table, try to ask someone sitting near you what he or she does or what brought them to the event. If there is an existing conversation going on at the table, you could try to find an opportunity to add something to what is being discussed if it does not sound personal or confidential.

BREAK INTO EXISTING CONVERSATIONS

In order to get the most out of networking events, you will need to break into some of the existing conversations so that you can meet as many people as possible at the event. However, this can seem intimidating and awkward, so here are four steps that you can follow to break into existing conversations:

Step 1—Approach the Edge of the Circle

If you see a group of people having a conversation, don't be afraid to walk right up to the group and stand just on the edge of their circle. As you do this, you can try to make eye contact, have a slight smile, and give a friendly nod if you make eye contact with someone in the circle.

When you do this, 50 percent of the time someone in the group will invite you into the conversation by asking how you are doing or what you do. If that happens, you can answer that person's questions and then ask the same question back. At this point, you should be part of the conversation and can ignore the remaining steps in this process.

Although, there will be times when the group continues talking and does not acknowledge you standing there. When that is the case, use the next step in the process.

Step 2—Apology and Explanation

You are standing at the edge of the group, and they are talking as though they don't know you are there. At this point, wait for the slightest pause in the conversation and politely interrupt by saying something this:

> *Hey, guys. I am sorry to interrupt. I haven't had a chance to meet you all yet, and I just wanted to introduce myself real quick.*

This is basically your conversation break-in opener.

Step 3—Introduction

From there, quickly transition to introducing yourself. Even though there are multiple people looking at you, you will start by introducing yourself to one person in the group. The easiest way to do is to turn to the person closest to you and say this:

> *I am [your name].* (Extend your hand for handshake.)

> (The person will likely respond with his or her name and shake your hand.)

At this point, try to notice if everybody in the group is paying attention to you or only the person you shook hands with. If it is only the person you shook hands with, follow up the handshake by asking that person what he or she does. You can follow that up with other networking questions directed primarily at that one person to try to establish a new one-on-one conversation on the side of the larger group conversation. However, if you have the attention of the full group when you are shaking hands with the first contact, you can try to get engaged with the full group, and that is explained in the next step.

Step 4—Rolling Introduction

After you shake hands with the first contact, move on to extend your hand and introduce yourself to the person to the left or right of the previous person you shook hands with. Repeat this to quickly go around the group until you shake everybody's hand and exchange names.

After you introduce yourself to everybody in the group, someone may ask you a question around what you do, and this will make you part of the conversation. If that does not happen, you can ask the question of "What do you do?" but direct it to the entire group by asking "What do you guys do?" From there, you will usually get a few answers back and you can either follow up by asking one of the people that answered with another question or they may ask you what you do and this exchange may lead to you being part of the group conversation.

DON'T JUDGE A BOOK BY ITS COVER

The last tip for getting into conversations is to not be picky about who you talk with. I say this because we can be quick to judge someone based on how the person looks, and this can factor into who we talk to when networking. For example, you may look at someone and think he or she is too young or too old to be a good prospect. Or you may think the person doesn't look like he or she has money or purchasing power.

This is not the optimum way of thinking for two reasons. First, your assumption could be totally wrong as you have no idea what is going on with someone, and you really should not judge a book by its cover. But more importantly, even if your read on someone is correct, this does not provide a reason to not talk to someone because your goal is to find networking partners, and these characteristics should not matter. Someone might not have money or power to purchase your product, but that does not mean that person does not have someone who does in his or her personal or professional network.

Post Event Tasks

When you get back to your office after attending a networking event, put all of the business cards you collected in a stack in front of you. Then go through this process for each card:

STEP 1—INVITE TO CONNECT ON LINKEDIN

Look up the contact on LinkedIn. If you are able to find them, send a customized connection invitation request with a mention of the event and anything memorable from your conversation if possible.

> Hi [Contact First Name],
>
> Great meeting you at [name of event]. I enjoyed our conversation and learning more about you.
>
> I look forward to possibly networking and collaborating with you in the future. Let's connect here on LinkedIn as a first step!
>
> Best Regards,
> [Your First Name]

STEP 2—SEND A FOLLOW-UP EMAIL

Send the contact a follow-up email to the email address on his or her business card. In this message, you can mention the event and anything memorable from your conversation if possible. You can also close for the next step in your sales process, which is setting up the Meeting sales step.

> Subject Line: Great meeting you!

> Hi [Contact First Name],

> Great meeting you at [name of event]. I enjoyed our conversation and would like to learn more about what you are doing.

> Are you interested in meeting for coffee so that we can continue our conversation?

> Best Regards,
> [Email Signature]

STEP 3—ADD CONTACT TO YOUR CRM

If you really want to build a strong relationship with a networking partner and stay in contact, add that person to your CRM and set tasks or reminders for yourself to check in with him or her periodically.

STEP 4—ADD CONTACT TO AN EMAIL CAMPAIGN

You want to try to do what you can to stay fresh in your networking partner's mind so that he or she continues to refer potential prospects to you. You can certainly do this by calling the partner and trying to get together periodically, but this can be time-consuming, and it can be easy to lose touch. With that being the case, one of the best ways to prevent networking partners from forgetting about you is to add them to your email marketing system so that they get some sort of automated email from you periodically.

CHAPTER 26

Prospecting on LinkedIn

LinkedIn is a great resource for finding and communicating with prospects. However, there are some small things you can do to get the most out of this valuable resource, and those are outlined in this chapter.

Searching for Prospects

LinkedIn is a great place to find prospects you can pursue, and you can use it in two different ways. First, if you have a territory that is more account-based with a list of target accounts, you can use LinkedIn to identify key people at the accounts you are trying to get into. All you have to do is run a search on the business name, and you will see every person who works there that has a LinkedIn profile. It is also extremely easy to refine your search to find people in particular locations, departments, etc.

If you have a territory that is more based on a particular geographic area, you can perform a search on your area in LinkedIn to identify businesses you can try to pursue. The nice thing about this process is that it will provide you with the names of businesses that you likely have never heard of and would not have known to reach out to without running a search on LinkedIn.

Reaching Out

Once you have found prospects that you want to contact, it is time to figure out how to reach out, and you have a few different options:

- Send an invitation to become LinkedIn connections
- Send an email message through LinkedIn
- Send an email outside of LinkedIn
- Call the prospect

INVITING TO BECOME CONNECTIONS

If you see a prospect on LinkedIn you want to sell to, you may think that the logical next step would be to send that person an invitation to become LinkedIn "connections." While this is probably the most common and popular choice for salespeople using LinkedIn, there are some good and bad things with this approach.

Three good things that happen when you become connections with your prospects are 1) you get access to any contact information he or she has added to their profile, 2) you will have the ability to send messages to this person through LinkedIn, and 3) you can broadcast updates and information through status updates that this person may see in his or her newsfeed.

The downside to becoming LinkedIn connections is that you should be a little more cautious about directly selling to the prospect. The is because an invitation to connect networks on LinkedIn is a friendly gesture, and if you follow that up immediately with an email selling your products, it can be seen as a bit rude or in bad taste. It is like inviting a friend over to your house and as soon as he or she arrives, you start trying to get him or her to sign up for something. Sure, you can invite a friend over and talk about something you are selling, but it would be best to do that after that person has been in your house for a while and not right after they walk through the door.

Converting that back to LinkedIn, if you become connections with a target prospect, try to have a buffer of time, messages, or conversations before trying to deliver your sales pitch. A good way to go is to try to start more of a networking conversation similar to what we discussed in Chapter 25, and transition to more of a sales pitch after that.

SENDING A MESSAGE THROUGH LINKEDIN

If you become connections with contacts, you can send messages directly to the contact's LinkedIn inbox. If you are not connections, you will have to use LinkedIn's InMail feature in order to send messages to contacts, and that will require a certain type of LinkedIn subscription level. The good thing about using the InMail feature in LinkedIn is that you can skip the invitation to connect step, which can not only save you steps and time, but you also don't have to worry about hitting the contact with your sales pitch right after becoming connections.

SEND EMAIL OUTSIDE OF LINKEDIN

Regardless of whether you send messages to the prospect on LinkedIn or not, you should send emails to a prospect's business email inbox. This is important because prospects are likely to pay more attention to their business email inbox than their LinkedIn inbox.

CALL THE PROSPECT

You always have the option to call prospects you find on LinkedIn. For prospects that you become connections with, you will be able to see any phone numbers they added to their profile. But if they do not have a phone number, simply go to the prospect's company website and call the main number and try to get routed to the contact through an operator or auto-attendant system.

What to Say When Reaching Out

We just outlined the different options that you have for reaching out. Now all you have to do is figure out what to say when you reach out. The good news is that you can use the same call scripts and email templates that were provided earlier in this book with some slight modifications, and I will outline all of that next. However, before we talk about what to do when you reach out, let's talk about some things to not do.

Don't Sound Like a Salesperson

There are two reasons that make it even more important to not sound like a salesperson when communicating with prospects on LinkedIn. First, the people that you want to pursue are likely getting messages from a lot of product selling salespeople. With that, if you reach out and sound like a salesperson who is trying to sell something, you increase the odds of being received in a negative way.

But another reason to try to not sound like a salesperson is that, while you might be on LinkedIn to sell your product, the people you are reaching out to are probably not on the platform looking to buy what you sell. In other words, LinkedIn is not a marketplace where buyers and sellers go to meet because the prospects are not buyers. What I mean by that is that the majority of people join LinkedIn to network, stay in touch with friends and colleagues, share ideas and information, advance their careers, and sell their own products. As a result, when they create a profile and accept an invitation to become connections, they are not doing all of that with the hope that someone will find them and try to sell them something. This does not mean that you cannot sell to people you find on LinkedIn. More so, this is just something you should be aware of and sensitive to when figuring out what best to say when you reach out.

The Instant Pitch

One of the biggest mistakes that I believe salespeople make on LinkedIn is that they do what I call the "Instant Pitch." This is where the salesperson sends an invite to connect and immediately after the contact accepts, the salesperson sends a product selling email. Here is an example of what this may look like:

Step 1—Invitation to Become Connections

The salesperson sends an invite to the prospect (me, for example) asking to become LinkedIn connections.

Hello Michael,

It looks like we have a lot of mutual connections. I would love to add you to my network!

Step 2—Invitation Accepted
I accept the invitation to become LinkedIn connections.

Step 3—Salesperson Sends Product Selling Message
Immediately after I accept the invitation, the salesperson then sends a product selling email like this:

> *Hello Michael,*
>
> *Thank you for accepting my invitation to connect! We provide accounting services. Are you looking to change tax and accounting firms? Are you available for a 15 to 20 minute call where I can tell you about the services we provide?*

I call this approach the "Instant Pitch" because the salesperson is instantly pitching what he or she sells right after becoming connections. To avoid doing an Instant Pitch, create a little buffer after the connection accept with either some time or messages. You can also decrease the Instant Pitch by using a networking message that is more around starting a networking partner type of conversation similar to what we discussed in the last chapter. If you focus on using more of a consultative selling message instead of a product selling sales message, this will also decrease how much you look like you are trying to sell something with an Instant Pitch.

Don't Make the Prospect Work
Salespeople often send a message asking a question that makes the prospect have to work in order to reply. Here are some examples of questions that put the prospect to work:

- *Tell me about your business.*
- *What are you biggest challenges?*
- *What do you do?*
- *What are you working on these days?*

To answer any of those questions in an email message would take a decent amount of thought, effort, and typing. Not only is it a little rude to ask questions that make the prospect work, but this type of message will have a much lower response rate.

If You Tailor Your Message, Really Try to Tailor Your Message

A lot of people on LinkedIn will tailor their connection invitation message, but they tailor the message with a canned message that could be sent to many different people. For example, people might say that the contact has an impressive profile, but they will not include any details as to why it is impressive. Or they will send a message mentioning having mutual connections, but they do not mention any of the common connections. Neither of these are horrible, but they could be seen as canned messages that are being sent to many different people. With that, why take the extra step to tailor the message to only use a canned message that is not tailored to the actual contact? A better way to do this is to take a quick look at the contact's profile and make a compliment or observation that is tailored to the actual person that the invitation is going to. Here are some examples:

- *Your background is interesting—you went from distribution to operations manager in just two years!*
- *You profile is impressive—23 years at XYZ Corp!*
- *We have a lot of mutual connections. You also worked with Michele Johnson?*

Don't Be "All About Me" in Your Messages

Try to not send messages that are all about you to contacts you find on LinkedIn. For example, salespeople often send messages on LinkedIn that are extensions of these thoughts:

- *This is who I work for.*
- *This is what we sell.*
- *This is what our products do.*
- *Do you need what I sell?*

- *Can I schedule a meeting to talk to you about buying my product?*

Not only is this bad because it is all about the salesperson's interests, but this is also not great because people on LinkedIn are likely not in buying mode for the product the salesperson sells. This will also make you look like a salesperson who is trying to sell something, which can increase the instant delete rate for your message.

Don't Use Too Many Words in Your Messages

As we discussed in Chapter 18 on email prospecting, it is important to use as few words as possible in your messages. This is even more important when sending emails to a prospect's LinkedIn inbox because emails are displayed in a very small window, and the prospect will have to scroll a lot more than he or she would in a business email inbox. This small window will make your emails look longer than they actually are, which means you need to be even more concerned with the word count when sending emails through LinkedIn.

LINKEDIN EMAIL MESSAGES

Figuring out what to say is fairly easy as you can just use your consultative selling sales message and all of the email templates in Chapter 12 for prospects that you find on LinkedIn. When you email contacts that you found on LinkedIn, it can be helpful to mention that you found them on LinkedIn by starting your email out with "I came across your profile on LinkedIn" to warm up the cold email. Here is what that looks like when added to the Cold Email - Value Points, and you can add this to the beginning of any of the cold email templates.

Subject Line: [Value Point]

Hello [Contact First Name],

I came across your profile on LinkedIn and I wanted to reach out because we help [Target Buyer Type] to:

- Value Point 1
- Value Point 2
- Value Point 3

I don't know if you want to improve those areas and that is why I am reaching out.

Are you available for a brief 15 to 20 minute meeting where I can share some examples of how we have helped other [Target Buyer Type] to [Value Point]?

Best Regards,
[Email Signature]

LINKEDIN CALL SCRIPTS

You can also use all of the call scripts outlined in Chapter 11 if you are treating the contacts you find on LinkedIn as prospects with little to no modifications. If you are going to treat them more as networking partners, the scripts would change a bit, and that is outlined below.

Networking Call Script for LinkedIn
Introduction

Hello, [Contact's Name]. This is [Your Name] from [Your Company]. We recently became connections on LinkedIn. Have I caught you in the middle of anything?

Recap

Great. The reason for my call is that I try to reach out to my connections on LinkedIn to learn about what they do to try to see if there are any ways that I can help them to be more successful.

Sales Takeaway

I actually don't know if you are interested in building new networking relationships, but that is why I am reaching out.

Close

Are interested in scheduling some time to talk in a little more detail? I would like to learn more about what you are doing and working on.

MEETING SCRIPT FOR LINKEDIN

When you reach the Meeting sales process step, you can use the First Appointment Script and the Networking Meeting Script that are provided in Chapter 15 with no modifications.

CHAPTER 27

Improving Mental Strength

The last area that we will discuss is improving your thoughts and mental strength. This is important because being a salesperson can be a rollercoaster ride with many highs and lows. If you do not have a certain level of mental strength, the level of stress can decrease how much you enjoy your job. If you reach a place where you aren't enjoying selling, you might end up not putting in as much activity as you should, which can negatively impact your overall sales performance. But the good news is that there are very small things that you can do to increase your mental strength, and I will discuss those in this chapter.

Decrease Self-Doubt

Maybe you are confident about what you are doing and never doubt yourself. But it would be very understandable for you to have moments when you doubt your skills or what you are doing due to all of the rejection, objections, and challenges that are part of a salesperson's daily life. Here are a few tips to decrease and control any feelings of self-doubt that you may experience.

DISMISS COMMON MISCONCEPTIONS

There are a few misconceptions that can have a negative impact on how you view yourself and the work you are doing.

You should enjoy what you do for a living.

It is a common belief that you should enjoy your job if you have picked a career that you are the right fit for. This is not a bad philosophy given how much of your life you spend working. But it might not be great to apply this to sales because prospecting, especially cold calling, can be grinding work that might not be a lot of fun. When you are fighting on the front lines and in the trenches, you might doubt if you are cut out for sales or if you have what it takes to be successful. Keep in mind that almost everybody feels discomfort and a lack of enjoyment when cold calling, so don't give up by thinking that the profession of sales is not for you.

Salespeople are born, not made.

There is a common belief that salespeople are born, and it is your personality and traits that will determine whether you can be a good salesperson or not. I do not agree with this as I believe that selling is a skill and one that can be learned and developed. Sure, you need some basic personality traits like the ability to communicate with other humans, an internal drive to be successful, and an ability to learn. But if you have those qualities at a minimum and you really want to be a salesperson, I believe that if you put in enough effort and energy, you can develop the skill of selling and be a successful salesperson.

You need to have a certain personality in order to sell.

Many people think that you need a certain type of personality in order to be a successful salesperson. Part of this belief is that you have to be very talkative with the "gift of gab," be gregarious, or be the loudest person in the room in order to sell and close. I completely disagree with this. In fact, if you can't tell from just about every chapter in this book, I believe the key to selling is asking good questions, and a big part of asking good questions is being a good listener. Many of the people who are big "talkers" are often not as good at asking questions and listening, and that could be more of a weakness when trying to be a consultative selling salesperson.

You need to be pushy and aggressive to be a good salesperson.

People often think a good salesperson will need to be pushy and aggressive. But if you sell in a way where you focus on finding prospects who need what you sell, if you clearly communicate how you can help, and if you lead prospects through a structured sales process, you can be a successful salesperson without being pushy and aggressive.

Be Aware of the External Environment

Trying to get your foot in the door of new accounts can be a grind, and this can make you doubt if you have what it takes to be successful. You might think that selling is difficult because of your level of skills and abilities, but a lot of it is because of the external environment that you are trying to operate in, and it has less to do with you than you think.

Prospects Are Extremely Busy

The prospects you are trying to sell to are extremely busy. And the higher you go in an organization, the busier prospects are. It is safe to assume that prospects have a million things going on in terms of meetings, requests, distractions, deadlines, etc. Because of this, it is tough to get their attention when calling and sending emails.

Tremendous Amount of Competition

There are a lot of salespeople calling and emailing the same prospects that you are, and everybody is competing for the same fixed bucket of time, attention, and money.

Prospects Do Not Answer Their Phones

Because of the first two points mentioned—prospects are extremely busy and have a lot of different people trying to get to them—they are often reluctant to answer their phones.

Prospects Put Gatekeepers in Your Way

Prospects will often use gatekeepers as a wall to block out salespeople who are trying to sell something.

Prospects Are Not in Buying Mode

When you do successfully make it through all of the obstacles and get connected with a target prospect, it is likely that he or she will not be in buying mode and could end up being difficult by giving you objections in order to try to get rid of you.

I share all of that again for two reasons. First, every salesperson is operating in this same external environment, so when you feel frustrated by some of these factors, keep in mind that everybody is dealing with the same challenges. The second thing is that there is nothing that you can do to change any of these factors. For example, you can't change the fact that a lot of salespeople are calling the same people that you are. But what you can do is become more aware of the environment and modify your approach so that you mitigate all of these challenges.

Be Aware of Your Internal Environment

There is also an internal environment that you can become more aware of, and this is what is going on in your head.

Fear of Rejection

Regardless of the situation, rejection is not fun and does not feel good. And in sales, it is pretty much guaranteed that you will have to experience a certain amount of rejection almost every day.

Call Reluctance

With rejection being a potential outcome of every cold call, it can be easy to feel reluctance when it is time to make cold calls.

Lack of Clarity for What to Do and Say

Conversations with prospects are often short and fast, and this can make it difficult to figure out the best thing to say and do.

Lack of Confidence

If it is not completely clear what to say and do, it can be easy for a salesperson to have a lack of confidence in certain sales situations such as cold calling, meeting with prospects, or delivering presentations.

Low Belief in Product

If salespeople experience a lot of rejection, they can begin to lose confidence in what they sell and forget why prospects should buy from them.

Lack of Motivation

If a salesperson has any of the things previously mentioned, this could have a negative impact on his or her motivation to perform sales prospecting activities like cold calling, email prospecting, networking, etc.

If you have any negative thoughts like these, they can not only impact your sales efforts, but they can also impact your life. The good news is that while you don't have much control over your external environment, you have a tremendous amount of control over your internal environment as there are a lot of small things you can do that can improve your thoughts and feelings, and we will outline some of those next.

BECOME MORE PREPARED

One of the biggest and easiest things you can do to improve your internal environment is to become more prepared. Here are all of the ways that being more prepared will help you:

- Decrease fear of rejection because you will know what to say when someone gives you objections

- Decrease the amount of rejection you get because you will sound better and make a better impression
- Improve confidence because you will know what to say and ask in all of the different situations that you will end up in
- Because you will have more confidence and know what to say, you will have less call reluctance

Here are three things that you can create at a minimum to help you improve your level of preparation:

1. Call scripts
2. Key questions to ask
3. Objection responses

Another thing that can greatly improve your level of preparation is to practice your pitch and how to handle certain situations through role-play exercises. You can work with a colleague, manager, or coach and try to practice common situations like cold calls, objection handling, meeting with prospects, delivering presentations, etc. Being able to work through these situations in a practice environment can drastically improve your level of preparation.

CHANGING YOUR MINDSET

It may sound a little far-fetched to imagine changing the way you think, but there are some very small and practical things that you can do to modify how you think and feel while selling and talking with prospects.

Value Awareness

If you are in more of a product selling mode and trying to talk prospects into wanting what you sell, it can be easy to have your product and its features primarily at the front of your mind. And with that type of mindset, you can feel like you are bugging prospects because you are interrupting them to talk about what you sell. But if you try to replace the product details that are in the front of your mind with all of the value points that your product provides, you can feel less like you are bugging and more like you are helping.

Making this change so that you think more about your value points is called increasing your value awareness, and it is basically staying aware of the value that your product has to offer. An example of how this can help you is that if your product helps to reduce employee injuries, by keeping this at the front of your mind, you will feel better about what you are trying to sell because preventing injuries is extremely helpful for both the employer and employees. With that detail in the front of your mind, you should feel more confident about calling your prospect because you have something that is very important and helpful to offer. Not only will keeping the value at the front of your mind help to improve your mindset, but it will also help you to remember to share your value points when you talk with prospects.

In order to become more value aware, you first have to have clarity around the value that your product offers, and that was discussed in Chapter 6 where we showed you a process for outlining the value that you offer. The next thing you will need to do is to remind yourself of that value periodically. For example, when you are about to call a prospect, you can stop yourself for a few seconds and think about all of the ways you could potentially help the prospect you are about to talk to.

View Yourself as a Giver

When you are in product selling mode, it can be easy to view yourself as a "taker"—you are calling prospects to initially take their time so that you can talk to them about your product. And ultimately, you want to take their money when you get them to buy what you are trying to sell. This type of thinking can make you feel like you are bothering the prospects you are pursuing, which is a weaker and more negative mindset.

To improve this, view yourself more as a giver than a taker. If you complete the previous tip of trying to stay more aware of the value that you have to offer, this should be easy because it is the ways your product helps that makes you a giver. If you sell a pill that helps someone to sleep better at night, instead of seeing the situation as you trying to sell your pill, view it as you are trying to help the prospect to improve his or her life by sleeping better at night.

Eliminate Weak Language

If a salesperson is operating more as a taker, he or she might feel less confident about the reason for contacting a prospect, and this can lead to the salesperson using weaker language than he or she should. For example, many salespeople will open a call or email by saying something similar to one the following:

- *I know you are busy right now.*
- *I will try to not take too much of your time.*
- *I am sorry to bother you.*
- *I will make this really quick.*

Try to eliminate using language like this when talking with your prospects. Not only does this make you look like a salesperson who is trying to sell something, but using this language can also be impacting your mindset.

You don't have to be apologetic when trying to start conversations with prospects. When you become more value aware and see yourself more as a giver than a taker, you will see that there is nothing wrong with calling prospects because you are trying to see if they are in the group of people or businesses that desperately need the help that you offer. You have nothing to apologize for and should not view yourself as being a bother. For example, if you found a wallet on the ground and you are trying to find the person who it belongs to, would you be apologetic when you approached people to see if they were missing their wallet? Would you worry about bothering them or taking them away from what they are doing? You probably would not because you know that what you have is of tremendous value. This same concept applies to your product as it offers tremendous value for the person who needs what you sell.

Sales Affirmations

This next tip may sound a bit fluffy, but there is a concept of using affirmations to improve your mindset. An affirmation is a positive statement that is a reminder of your strengths or something good in your life. Having these reminders can be helpful because we often think about our problems, weaknesses, or what is not going well and sometimes completely forget what is good. If you focus more on the negative stuff in your life, you will have a more negative mindset. And if you think more about the positive, you will have a more positive mindset.

Using affirmations is simply a tool and process to help you to focus more on what is good in order to shift toward a more positive and stronger mindset. One way to apply this to selling is to use affirmations to improve your mindset through the ups and downs that come with being a salesperson. For example, when you have feelings of frustration, anxiety, doubt, fear, or disappointment, you can use affirmations to minimize how much those emotions impact you.

This could help you if you have anxiety when performing phone prospecting. Not only can anxiety about making calls impact how you sound on the phone, but it can also decrease the number of calls you end up making. One option here is to use your value points as a sales affirmation to make you feel better about your reason for contacting the prospect. The way to apply that would be to reflect on all of the great improvements that your product can make before you start your prospecting or before each call. This will also help you to become more value aware and help you to view yourself as more of a giver than a taker.

Using Your Sales Message as Affirmations

Each component of the consultative selling sales message can be used as sales affirmations:

- **Value Points:** You can use the improvements your product offers to increase your confidence in what you sell and feel more justification for reaching out to prospects.

- **Pain Points:** You can use the problems that your product helps to solve to remind yourself that there are people out there who truly need what you sell.

- **Name-Drop:** Customer examples are great affirmations to remind you that there are people out there who need your product.

- **Product:** The ways your product differs from the competition and the ROI your product delivers could be used to remind yourself as to why your product is better than the competition and why your prospect should want to talk with you.

The practice of using affirmations does not need to be complicated. You can simply create the affirmations that you think are helpful for you and put them on a piece of paper. You can put this piece of paper on your wall in your office or leave it on your desk. Then simply look at them when you start your day or when you are in prospecting mode. One side benefit from using sales affirmations that are derived from your sales message is that this will put your sales message at the front of your mind, helping you to remember the key points you need to make when talking with prospects.

ALTERNATIVE MINDSET IMPROVEMENT ACTIVITIES

Here are a few things you can do to improve your mindset that are outside of your daily sales responsibilities.

Meditation
Meditation is probably one of the best things you can add to your life to improve your mindset. Incorporating some amount of mediation into your daily routine can not only improve your mindset when selling, but it can also change and improve how you think in all areas of your life.

Yoga
Adding some amount of yoga to your daily or weekly routine can be a great way to release both physical and mental stress.

Reading
Using the activity of leisure reading is a good way a good way to calm down your mind. Depending on your job and routine, you might be able to find small moments during the day to take a break from the madness by reading

for a few minutes. Or you can use this at the end of the day before you go to sleep as a way to quiet and relax your mind.

Reboot with a Nap

Many people view taking naps as being lazy and having a negative impact on productivity. But when used the right way, naps can improve your mindset and increase your productivity. The key to this is the length of time that you nap for. If you take a nap that is between ten to twenty minutes, it is similar to when you reboot your computer as you will usually wake up refreshed with a clearer mind. Being able to refresh your mind in this way will often help to increase your overall productivity for the day by helping you to work better and longer than you would if you did not get a mental break.

However, if you sleep longer than twenty minutes, you are more likely to go into a deeper level of sleep, and you can wake up feeling tired. In this scenario, not only did you lose productivity during the nap, but you might have less productivity for the rest of the day. As you can see, naps can be helpful, but it is a delicate balance and you have to get it right in order to have a positive effect.

Exercise

One of the best ways to release stress is to exercise in some way or another. If you don't currently have any type of exercise routine, adding this can be one of the best ways to improve your mindset. Not only does exercising release endorphins that will make you feel better and relieve stress, but exercising increases blood flow to the brain. Having more blood flow to your brain can only be a good thing, right?

Walk

Incorporating some amount of time into your daily routine for a walk is a great way to take a mental break to decompress. Daily walking is also an excellent form of exercise. You can either use your walks as a place to think about your sales efforts to plan out your next moves, or you can take a complete break and think about anything that is not related to selling.

The nice thing about taking walks is that you can just about do them any-where. Regarding timing, you could do morning walks before you go to work, midmorning, after lunch, or in the evening when you get home. Nothing real complex about how to incorporate this—just try to periodically stop what you are doing and take a walk.

Maintaining Mental Strength

Here are some tips that can help you to maintain mental strength and motivation moving forward.

COMPARTMENTALIZE YOUR TIME

The daily life of a salesperson can be chaotic with a lot of pressure and many differ-ent tasks that need to be completed. This can create a lot of stress if you don't have the right level of organization in place. One thing you can do to minimize the chaos and stress is to compartmentalize your day and week to create segments of time for the different categories of tasks that you need to work on. For example, you can cre-ate windows of time for cold calling, administrative tasks, sales training, networking, customer calls, etc.

The way to apply this is that during a particular block of time, you will stop every-thing else that you have to do and only focus on the category of tasks that you have designated for that time. This focus can not only help you to stay on top of completing what you need to do, but it can also help you to decrease stress by having more clarity and control for what you need to work on.

ESTABLISH A DAILY ROUTINE

Establishing more of a daily structure and routine can help you to stay focused and motivated. This could include creating more structure around the time that you start your day, the times that you work on different activities, the order with which you perform certain types of tasks, etc. For example, a salesperson who works from home might not have anyone watching to make sure he or she is working and staying productive. With that freedom, it can be easy to lose motivation and focus. One tactic to minimize that challenge is to establish a daily routine where the salesperson starts working at the same time every day and even gets dressed like he or she is going into an office. This routine could help a work-at-home salesperson to stay productive and minimize the chances of getting distracted or losing motivation.

CREATE YOUR OWN TARGETS

Establishing a strong mindset is not just about mitigating negative emotions and feelings; it is also about maintaining focus, drive, and competitiveness. A process that you can use for that is to set targets for yourself.

Sales Goals

If you are a salesperson working for a company, you likely have some sort of sales targets. But even if you already have an assigned quota or sales targets, the quotas that are assigned to salespeople are usually a big number spread across a long period of time (i.e., annual sales quota). What you can do is either take your annual quota, or the amount that you want to sell for the year, and break it down so that you have sales goals for the week, month, or quarter.

Activity Goals

Another thing you can do is create activity goals for yourself. These are for the activities that you need to perform in order to generate leads and sales. For example, if you have to perform activities like making calls, sending emails, going to events, meeting with prospects, and sending proposals in order to fill your pipeline, you can set goals for these activities for each day, week, or month. In theory, if you do a good job of identifying what activities you need to complete that will lead to closed business and you make good assumptions on how many of those you need to complete, then you will have clarity for what you need to do each day, week, and month in order to hit your sales goals.

TRACK PROGRESS

One way to increase your motivation is to track your activities and progress. Not only can this help with motivation by giving you a feeling of accomplishment, but this can also help you to make sure that you are on track with doing what you need to do to hit and exceed your sales targets. For example, you could track how many calls you make, how many meetings you schedule, how many demos you deliver, etc. You do not need to be sophisticated with how you do this as it could be as simple as a spreadsheet or a piece of paper with a checkmark each time an activity is completed. However, the more digital you can make your progress tracking, the more things you can do with your activity data. For example, the SalesScripter software application makes it extremely easy to document all of your different sales activities like calls made, emails sent, voicemails left, meetings completed, etc. Since we have all of that activity data in a central database, we can easily produce all sorts of charts that display what you are doing and accomplishing. This data can either be used with managing yourself or managing a sales team, helping you to figure out what you need to increase or change in order to hit your sales targets.

About the Author

If you are curious about where all of this comes from, this is some of the story that lead to me creating the SMART Sales System.

Discovering a Love for Sales

During my freshman year in college, I subscribed to a club that would send you music CDs every month. The club had a referral program and would give you three free CDs for every person you got to join the club. Being a broke college kid who loved music, I found this opportunity really cool and ended up getting about half of the dorm that I lived in to join the club, netting me about 150 free CDs.

I found that whole experience of getting people signed up for the music club to be extremely fun. Not only did I love getting free CDs in the mail after signing someone up, but I also enjoyed the process of finding a new prospect, telling that person about the program, building interest, getting around objections, and closing the deal. This is when I started to become interested in the profession of selling.

A Passion for Training

During the last few years of college, I worked at a restaurant as a server and bartender. After working at the restaurant for about a year, I started to think about how there was not a training process for new servers. I decided to take the initiative to create a four-day training program that broke out all of the different things new servers would need to learn and do. I shared the training program with management, and they ended up implementing the program exactly as I had built it and put me in charge of training all new servers. Taking this initiative certainly worked out well for my career at that restaurant in terms of my status, but the other benefit was that I thoroughly enjoyed working with the new servers to teach them all of the things they needed to know. It was then that I realized that I had a passion in the area of training.

Sales Systems Can Always Be Optimized

My first job out of college was working in inside sales at Compaq Computer Corporation. I was extremely lucky to get a job that allowed me to learn so much and gain such great experience. After working at Compaq for about a year, I realized that management was putting a lot of emphasis on training and compensating the department I was working in to sell more. Which is pretty standard, but the problem that I saw was that I was spending about 75 percent of my time working on customer service issues. It occurred to me that if the company wanted me to sell more and use all of the training they kept putting me through, if they split my current areas of responsibility into two different jobs—one that focused on sales and another that focused on resolving customer service issues—not only would the organization sell more, it would also probably provide better customer service.

With that thought, I took a similar initiative to what I did at the restaurant and wrote up a reorganization plan outlining how and why to break the department into two different groups—sales and customer service. I sent this document to my manager, and this time I only got a nice pat on the back for sharing my ideas. Not only that, but I actually heard that management laughed about me submitting this feedback in a meeting with comments like "Who does this kid think he is?" However, about six months after I shared my feedback, the department I was working in was reorganized into two separate groups: one for sales and one for customer service. Without worrying too much about whether or not it was my feedback that led to such a big reorganization, one thing I was sure about was that the area of sales consulting and optimizing sales organizations was extremely interesting to me.

It Is All about Asking Good Questions

While I started my career selling computers, I did not truly learn about selling until I worked in the software industry and when I worked as a sales rep for BMC Software.

Software sales can be challenging because you are selling something that people cannot see and feel, and sometimes they do not even know that they need what you sell. It is all about communicating the value in terms of what the software can improve and the problems it can help to resolve.

One thing I really came to terms with when selling software was that a key to success is asking the right questions. I remember having a good call and going to share it with my manager to give him the good news and run down. In most of these debriefings, my manager would ask me questions about the prospect that I often would not know the answer to. For example, my manager would ask if the prospect was the decision maker, or if the budget had been approved, or what was not great about the prospect's current system. I would think to myself how those were great questions, and I wished I would have known or remembered to ask those.

After going through this a few times, I started making notes of good questions to ask and put them in a spreadsheet that evolved into a sales tool that outlined different things to ask and talk about with prospects. This spreadsheet turned out to be a very helpful sales tool that helped me to improve my sales performance and I ended up sharing it with a number of different colleagues. They loved it and would routinely come back to me asking for the latest version or if there were any updates. Now that I look back, I really enjoyed creating that sales tool and helping other salespeople to sell more. You could probably say that this spreadsheet was the very first version of the SalesScripter software application and my teammates were my first customers.

Changing the Buyer Changes the Message

As my sales career progressed, I moved on to a sales role at Kronos selling workforce management software. It was this experience that really helped me to realize that it can help to use different messages for different buyer personas.

The product I sold was fairly straightforward in that it helped businesses with timekeeping and scheduling for their employees. I sold to retail businesses, hospitals, and manufacturers. And while each customer I sold to basically used the same product, when I looked at the three different types of buyers I was selling to, they each had completely different employees. Retail businesses have a lot of part-time employees; hospitals have employees with many different skills and certifications, creating very complex scheduling challenges; and manufacturers have a lot of complexity around unions and blue collar workers. What all of that means is that while I was selling the same product to all of these different buyers, in order for me to communicate clearly and build the most interest, I needed to talk about and focus on each buyer's unique needs and interests. It was then that I realized that when you change the buyer you are selling to, your sales pitch should also change.

Earning My Stripes

After being a salesperson for about thirteen years, I realized that I wanted to create my own sales consulting practice. But I knew that I needed to gain a little more experience before taking that step, so I took a sales role working for Ceridian and sold payroll outsourcing services. I chose this position because I knew that selling payroll outsourcing would be extremely challenging, and this would really help me to refine my skills and build on all of the things I had already learned. Ceridian also provided a rigorous thirteen-week sales training program, and I knew that the training and experience in this role would be a great bootcamp for me right before I started my consulting practice.

During my time at Ceridian, I was forced to go back to the basics and spent every day working in trenches generating my own leads through cold calling, cold emailing, and networking. It is actually my experience selling payroll outsourcing that helped me to develop the objection handling methodology that is central to the SMART Sales System approach.

One Thing Usually Leads to Another

After leaving Ceridian, I started a sales consulting business called Launch Pad Solutions. I focused primarily on sales consulting for small businesses, and I found that most of my clients wanted help with cold calling and outbound prospecting. After about 6 months, I realized that if I had a team of cold callers, I could sell that as a service to my clients in the form of appointment setting or cold call outsourcing. With that realization, I purchased a cloud VoIP phone system, subscribed to a web-based CRM application, and hired a team of work-at-home agents creating a virtual cold call outsourcing operation. I ended up selling much more cold call outsourcing than sales consulting and that turned out to be the primary service that we provided at Launch Pad Solutions.

Developing the SMART Sales Methodology

As I hired work-at-home agents, I needed to train them on my approach to cold calling. As a result, I started creating recorded training modules on all of the key concepts that I wanted them to know: cold calling, cold emailing, asking questions, finding pain, building interest, dealing with objections, getting around gatekeepers, managing the sales process, closing, etc. After I created all of those training modules, I thought all of these tips would make a good sales training book, so I wrote and published *The Cold Calling Equation—PROBLEM SOLVED* in 2012. That book and all of those training modules were the first version of the SMART Sales System.

Pursuing a Unique Idea

When clients hired us to do their cold calling, I had to create scripts, emails, voicemails, and objection responses for their cold callers. In order to create all of those documents, I would interview my clients to ask a series of questions. After going through that process again and again, I had the idea that I could create a piece of software that would have all of the questions that I asked my clients and then link all of the answers to the templates of scripts and emails that I was creating for each project. If my idea would work, a salesperson or manager could answer the questions in the software, and the software would create all of his or her documents and function as a sales script-writing software application.

I did a search on the internet, and nothing like that existed, so I had it built. In January of 2013, we launched the first version of SalesScripter. While it started as a sales script builder, we have focused on continuing to develop and improve the application and have added functionality in the areas of CRM, email automation, sales training, sales recruiting, and more. Today, we have grown to have customers around the globe who are using our software to either improve their own sales efforts or to train and improve their sales team.

Focused on Making Salespeople SMARTer

We combined SalesScripter with our sales training methodology to create the SMART Sales System, and that is what we focus on today. We provide salespeople with sales training, sales consulting, sales coaching, and the SalesScripter software application, and all of these are focused on helping to make salespeople SMARTer so that they can improve their sales results, increase their income, and improve their lives.

Additional Resources

Sales Training

If you would like to access more of our sales training materials, there are couple of options. First, you can visit our YouTube channel where you will find hundreds of training videos that you can watch for free. There are so many that it can be easy to get lost or to not know which video to watch. We have tried to help you with this by creating different playlists of videos. Look for these as there will be different sets of training videos packaged together and that will make it easy for you to work through them in a logical manner.

While we provide most of our training on YouTube for free, we certainly provide live sales training for both virtual and in-person audiences. The really nice thing about our live training and the SMART Sales System is that, if a company hires us to train their salespeople, we can go through the process in Section 1 of this book with the client to create their consultative selling sales message. This message can then be used to create all of the documents and tools provided in Section 2 of this book. We can then customize all of the training modules in Section 3 by using their sales message for all of the examples and explanations. With that, when we teach the concept of value, we use the value points from the client's sales message. When we teach asking questions, we use the questions from the client's sales message. This makes these live training sessions tailored to the audience and much more productive compared to discussing the topics using random examples.

SalesScripter Software Application

If you like the SMART Sales System and our overall sales methodology, you might want to check out the SalesScripter software application because it completely aligns with everything discussed in this book and taught in our sales training modules. Visit www. salesscripter.com for more information on SalesScripter.

Sales Consulting

We are available to help salespeople and businesses to build their sales strategy and message. If we work with you helping to build your sales message, we can either work with you outside of the SalesScripter software application or we can build your message in the software. A lot of customers will sign up for SalesScripter and then purchase a few hours of consulting. With that combination, we can go through the software with the customer and help them to answer all of the questions in order to create their sales message. This process is always extremely productive and at the end of it, the customer will have their account loaded up with a very good sales message. That sales message will then be used by the software to populate their library of scripts, emails, and templates. With that, after just a couple of consulting hours, our customers basically get a library of documents that is written and created by us.

Made in the USA
Monee, IL
12 August 2020